3

ScottForesman

Accelerating English Language Learning

Authors

Anna Uhl Chamot

Jim Cummins

Carolyn Kessler

J. Michael O'Malley

Lily Wong Fillmore

Consultant

George González

ScottForesman

Editorial Offices: Glenview, Illinois

Regional Offices: Sunnyvale, California • Atlanta, Georgia

Glenview, Illinois • Oakland, New Jersey • Dallas, Texas

ACKNOWLEDGMENTS

Illustrations Unless otherwise acknowledged, all illustrations are the property of Scott, Foresman and Company. Page abbreviations are as follows: (T) top, (B) bottom, (L) left, (R) right, (C) center.

Elizabeth Allen **188–189**, **228**, **230–236**; Ka Botzis **48–49**, **104–105**, **196–197**; Lee Lee Brazeal **114**; John Burgoyne **116–117**, **160–161**, **178–179**, **200–201**, **212–213**; Patrice Rossi Calkin **162–163**, **198**, **205**; Ruta Daugavietis **12**, **13**, **76**; Paul Dolan **24–25**, **38**, **100**, **182–183**; Ebet Dudley **120–121**; Lane Dupont **9**, **15**, **52**, **54**, **55**, **56**, **57**; Kate Brennan Hall **26–37**; Brian Karas **176**; Laura Kelly **2–3**, **16–17**; Todd Leonardo **107**, **192–193**, **204**; Mary Morgan **64–75**; Mapping Specialists **22–23**, **146–147**, **200–201**; Anita Nelson **122–123**; Gary Phillips **14**, **194–195**; Ruben Ramos **88**, **90–91**, **93**, **94–95**, **96–97**, **98**; John Sandford **20–21**, **42–43**, **46–47**, **78–79**, **124–125**, **184–185**, **186–187**; Joel Spector **138**, **158–159**, **214–215**; Susan Spellman **4–5**, **82–83**, **150–151**, **152**, **190**, **216–227**; Three Communication Design **84**, **85**.

Literature 26–37: "City Mouse and Country Mouse" by Jane Buxton. First published in the NEW ZEALAND SCHOOL JOURNAL, Part 2, Number 2, 1988. Copyright © 1988 by Jane Buxton. Reprinted by permission of the author. **64–75**: From the book SINGING BIRDS AND FLASHING FIREFLIES by Dorothy Hinshaw Patent, illustrated by Mary Morgan, pages 3-6, 10-15, and 31. Text copyright © 1989 by Dorothy Hinshaw Patent. Illustrations copyright © 1989 by Mary Morgan. All rights reserved. Reprinted by permission of the publisher, Franklin Watts, Inc. **88–99**: "Minnie the Mambo Mosquito" by Carmen Tafolla. Copyright © 1991 by Carmen Tafolla. **126–137**: From "Desert Animals" from the book DESERTS by Elsa Posell, pages 13-15, 18, 20-21, and 22-25. Copyright © 1958 by Elsa Posell. All rights reserved. Reprinted by permission of the publisher, Childrens Press. **164-175**: HOUSES AND HOMES by Ann Morris. Copyright © 1992 by Ann Morris. Reprinted by permission of Lothrop, Lee and Shepard Books, a division of William Morrow and Company, Inc. **216–227**: "Linda's Invention" by Dina Anastasio from RAINBOW SHOWER. Copyright © 1983 by Scott, Foresman and Company.

Poems and Songs 14: Adapted from "Pick a Bale of Cotton" by Tom Glazer. Original adaptation and arrangement by Tom Glazer. Copyright © 1964, renewed © 1992 by Songs Music, Inc. Reprinted by permission of Songs Music, Inc. **38**: "Sing a Song of Cities" from GOOD RHYMES, GOOD TIMES by Lee Bennett Hopkins. Copyright © 1974, 1995 by Lee Bennett Hopkins. Reprinted by permission of Curtis Brown Ltd. **52**: "The Park" by James S. Tippett from CRICKETY CRICKET!: THE BEST LOVED POEMS OF JAMES S. TIPPETT. Copyright 1993, copyright renewed © 1973 by Martha K. Tippett. Reprinted by permission of HarperCollins Publishers, Inc. **76**: "Lightning Bugs" by Erika Northrop from HUMPTY DUMPTY'S MAGAZINE, March 1995, Volume 43, Number 2, Page 48. Copyright © 1995 by Children's Better Health Institute, Benjamin Franklin Literary & Medical Society, Inc. Reprinted by permission of Children's Better Health Institute, Benjamin Franklin Literary & Medical Society, Inc., Indianapolis, Indiana. **100**: "Ears Hear" from OODLES OF NOODLES by Lucia M. and James L. Hymes, Jr. Copyright © 1964 by Lucia M. and James L. Hymes, Jr. Reprinted by permission of Addison-Wesley Publishing Company, Inc. **138**: "The Desert" by Eucario Mendez. Copyright © 1990 by Eucario Mendez. Reprinted by permission of the author. **150-152**: "My Mother's Got Me Bundled Up" from IT'S SNOWING! IT'S SNOWING! by Jack Prelutsky, pages 32-34. Copyright © 1984 by Jack Prelutsky. Reprinted by permission of Greenwillow Books, a division of William Morrow and Company, Inc. **176**: "Houses" from UP THE WINDY HILL by Aileen Fisher. Reprinted by permission of the author. **190**: "Let's Build a House" by Lucille Wood from SING A SONG OF PEOPLE by Roberta McLaughlin and Lucille Wood, page 47. Copyright © 1973 by BOWMAR®. All rights reserved. Reprinted by permission of Warner Bros. Publications U.S. Inc., Miami, FL 33014. **228**: "Danger Sign" from EARTH LINES by Pat Moon. Copyright © 1993 by Pat Moon. Reprinted by permission of Greenwillow Books, a division of William Morrow and Company, Inc.

Photography Unless otherwise acknowledged, all photographs are the property of Scott, Foresman and Company. Page abbreviations are as follows: (T) top, (C) center, (B) bottom, (R) right.

v(t, b) Superstock; **4**(t), **4–5**, **6**(tc, bc, b), **7**(tl, bl), **8**(b, c) Superstock, Inc.; (t) James L. Shaffer/PhotoEdit; **9**(b) J. Gordon Miller/Superstock, Inc.; (t) Superstock, Inc.; **18**(b) Don Smetzer/Tony Stone Images; (c) Mark Richards/PhotoEdit; (t) Jeff Greenberg/PhotoEdit; **19**(l, r) Superstock, Inc.; **24** Don Smetzer/Tony Stone Images; **39**, **40–41**(background), **41**(t) Superstock, Inc.; **43**(bl) Okoniewski/Image Works; (br) Kevin Laubacher/FPG International; **44**(bl) Tony Stone Images; (bc) Mary Evans Picture Library; (br) Courtesy General Electric; (t) U.S.Department of the Interior, National Park Service, Edison Historic Site; **45**(bl) Superstock, Inc.; (br) Hughes Aircraft Company/Carl Byoir & Assoc., Inc.; (bc) Corbis-Bettmann; **50**(t) Peter Edes/Tony Stone Images; **80** Tony Freeman/PhotoEdit; **84**(r) Superstock, Inc.; (l) Jeff Greenberg/PhotoEdit; **85**(l, r) Superstock, Inc.; **102**(t) Superstock, Inc.; (c) Bonnie Kamin/PhotoEdit; (b) Ron Kimball; **103**(tl, br) Superstock, Inc.; (tr) Myrleen Ferguson/PhotoEdit; (bl) Ron Kimball; **106**(l, r), **107**, **118**, **119** Superstock, Inc.; **120** Peter Pearson/Tony Stone Images; **125** Nancy Sheehan/PhotoEdit; **126**(l) Superstock, Inc., (r) Rod Planck/Tony Stone Images; **126–127**(background) Willard Clay/Tony Stone Images; **126**, **127**(l) Tom Ulrich/Tony Stone Images; **127**(r), **128** Superstock, Inc.; **129** James P. Rowan/Tony Stone Images; **130** Rod Planck/Tony Stone Images; **131** James Simon/Tony Stone Images; **132–133** Superstock, Inc.; **134** M.A.Chappell/Animals Animals; **135** Tom Ulrich/Tony Stone Images; **136** Rod Planck/Tony Stone Images; **137** Superstock, Inc.; **140**(tr,bl,br) Superstock, Inc.; **141**(br) Gary Benson/Tony Stone Images; (t) Superstock, Inc.; (bl), **142**(t) Michael Newman/ PhotoEdit, (c) Superstock, Inc., (b) Felicia Martinez/PhotoEdit; **142–143**(background) Superstock, Inc.; **143**(t) Superstock, Inc.; (b) Robert Frerck/Odyssey Productions; **144–145** (background) Superstock, Inc.; **144**(t) Superstock, Inc., (c) Paul Conklin/ PhotoEdit, (b) Richard Hutchings/ PhotoEdit; **145**(b) Cosmo Condina/Tony Stone Images; (t) Superstock, Inc.; **148**(t) David Young-Wolff/PhotoEdit; **149**(t) Superstock, Inc.; **154**(b) Superstock, Inc.; (t) Michael Newman/PhotoEdit; **155**(tl,bl,r) Superstock, Inc.; **156**(br) Superstock, Inc.; (tl) Thane/Animals Animals/Earth Scenes, (tr) Johnny Johnson/AlaskaStock, (bl) Randy Brandon/ AlaskaStock; **157**(tl, tr, c, b) Superstock, Inc.; **164–175** Ken Heyman; **180**(tl) Don and Pat Valenti; (tr) Superstock, Inc.; **181**(tl) Maxwell Mackenzie/Tony Stone Images; (bl) Phil Degginger/Tony Stone Images;**183**(tl) David Young-Wolff/PhotoEdit; **206**(b) Mark Lewis/Tony Stone Images; **206–207** (background) Superstock, Inc.; **207** Ed Pritchard/Tony Stone Images, (t) Superstock, Inc.; **208**(r) Jeremy Walker/Tony Stone Images, (l) Superstock, Inc.; **209**(l) Andy Sacks/Tony Stone Images, (r) John Edwards/Tony Stone Images.

ISBN: 0-673-19670-4

Scott, Foresman and Company, Glenview, Illinois

4 5 6 7 8 9 10 KR 05 04 03 02 01 00 99 98 97

CRITIC READERS

Sandra H. Bible
Elementary ESL Teacher
Shawnee Mission School District
Shawnee Mission, Kansas

Betty A. Billups
Dallas Independent School District
Dallas, Texas

María G. Cano
BIL/ESL Specialist
Pasadena Independent School District
Pasadena, Texas

Anaida Colón-Muñiz, Ed.D.
Director of English Language Development and Bilingual Education
Santa Ana Unified School District
Santa Ana, California

Debbie Corkey-Corber
Educational Consultant
Williamsburg, Virginia

Lily Pham Dam
Instructional Specialist
Dallas Independent School District
Dallas, Texas

María Delgado
Edison Middle School
Milwaukee Public Schools
Milwaukee, Wisconsin

Dr. M. Viramontes de Marín
Chair, Education/ Liberal Arts Departments
The National Hispanic University
San Jose, California

Timothy Hart
Supervisor of English as a Second Language
Wake County
Raleigh, North Carolina

Lilian I. Jezik
Bilingual Resource Teacher
Colorna-Norco Unified School District
Norco, California

Helen L. Lin
Chairman, Education Program
Multicultural Arts Council of Orange County, California
Formerly ESL Lab Director, Kansas City, Kansas, Schools

Teresa Montaño
United Teachers Los Angeles
Los Angeles, California

Loriana M. Novoa, Ed.D.
Research and Evaluation Consultants
Miami, Florida

Rosa María Peña
Austin Independent School District
Austin, Texas

Thuy Pham-Remmele
ESL/Bilingual K–12 Specialist
Madison Metropolitan School District
Madison, Wisconsin

Roberto San Miguel
Kennedy-Zapata Elementary School
El Cenizo, Texas

Jacqueline J. Servi Margis
ESL and Foreign Language Curriculum Specialist
Milwaukee Public Schools
Milwaukee, Wisconsin

Elizabeth Streightoff
ESL Magnet Teacher, Lamar Elementary School
Conroe Independent School District
The Woodlands, Texas

Lydia M. Trujillo
Hot Topics Consultants
Pueblo, Colorado

Susan C. VanLeuven
Poudre R-1 School District
Fort Collins, Colorado

Rosaura Villaseñor, M.A.
Educator
Norwalk, California

Sharon Weiss
ESL Consultant
Glenview, Illinois

Cheryl Wilkinson
J. O. Davis Elementary School
Irving Independent School District
Irving, Texas

Phyllis I. Ziegler
ESL/Bilingual Consultant
New York, New York

TABLE OF CONTENTS

CHAPTER 1

Life on a Farm

Tell what you know.

Have you ever been on a farm?

What do you see on this farm?

Word Bank

barn
chickens
cows
farmer
farmhouse
field
pigs
tractor

Talk About It

How is this farm different from where you live? How is it the same?

What do farmers do?

There are many jobs to do on a farm. Everyone in the family helps.

Some farmers grow ▶ **crops.** Farmers grow fruits, vegetables, or grains by planting seeds.

◀ Farmers make sure their crops have plenty of water to help them grow. When the crops are ripe, the farmers **harvest** them to eat or sell.

Some farmers raise animals. They make sure their animals have plenty of food and water to help them grow.

Some farm animals can live outdoors. Other animals need a **shelter,** such as a barn or a pen. Farmers work hard to keep the shelters clean.

Think About It

Do you think it is harder to raise crops or animals? Why?

What kind of work would you like to do on a farm?

Why are farms important?

The fruits and vegetables people eat are grown on farms. The bread and cereal people eat come from grains that are grown on farms.

The milk people drink comes from cows that are raised on farms. Most of the meat people eat comes from cattle, turkeys, chickens, and pigs that are raised on farms.

▲ cow

▲ turkey

▲ chicken

▲ pig

▲ cotton

Many other things people need are grown on farms. Cotton is a plant. Farmers grow cotton and sell it. People use cotton to make cloth.

▲ sheep

Farmers raise sheep for their wool. They cut off the sheep's wool and sell it. People use wool to make cloth.

Write About It

Make a list of things you ate or used today that came from farms.

Growing Wheat

Wheat is an important grain. People eat breads, cereals, and many other foods made from wheat every day.

Farmers in Kansas grow a lot of wheat. Kansas has cold winters and warm summers. This weather is good for raising wheat.

In late summer or early fall, farmers plow fields and plant wheat seeds.

In fall, the wheat plants start to grow.

In winter, the snow protects the young wheat plants from the cold.

4

In spring, the snow melts. Water from the melted snow helps the wheat grow tall.

5

In summer, farmers use machines to harvest the wheat.

Word Bank

cake

crackers

muffins

noodles

tortillas

Think About It

Think about the foods you eat. Which are made from wheat?

Would the area where you live be a good place to grow wheat? Why or why not?

What is the temperature?

Farmers need to know what the **temperature** is. The temperature tells how warm or cold the air is.

A **thermometer** gives the temperature. It has a thin tube with liquid in it. As air warms, the liquid moves up the tube. As air cools, the liquid moves down the tube.

Look at the thermometers. Which one shows that the air is cooler?

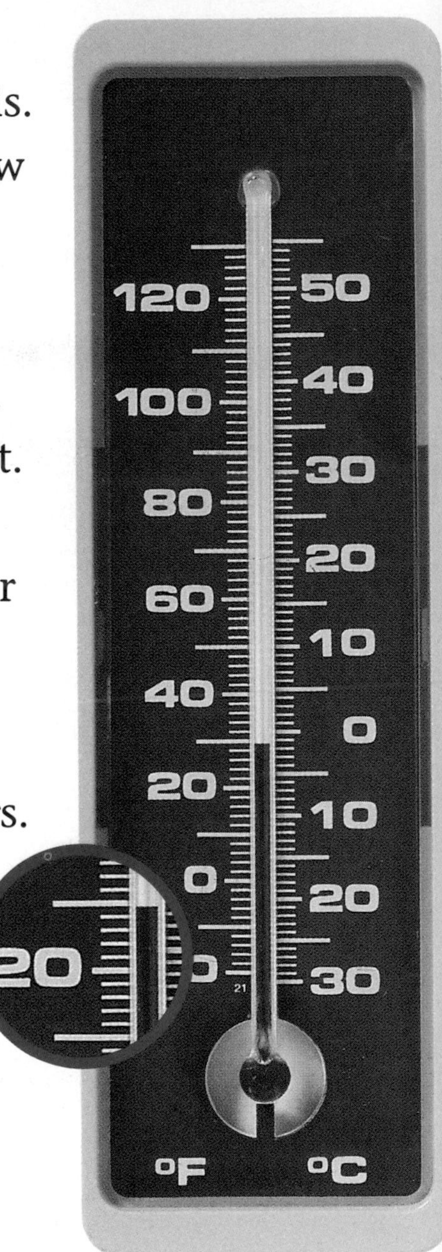

Measure the temperature.

Things You Need

thermometer

Follow these steps.

1. Put a thermometer inside your classroom for ten minutes.
2. After ten minutes, read the temperature on the thermometer.
3. Put the thermometer outside for ten minutes.
4. After ten minutes, read the temperature on the thermometer.

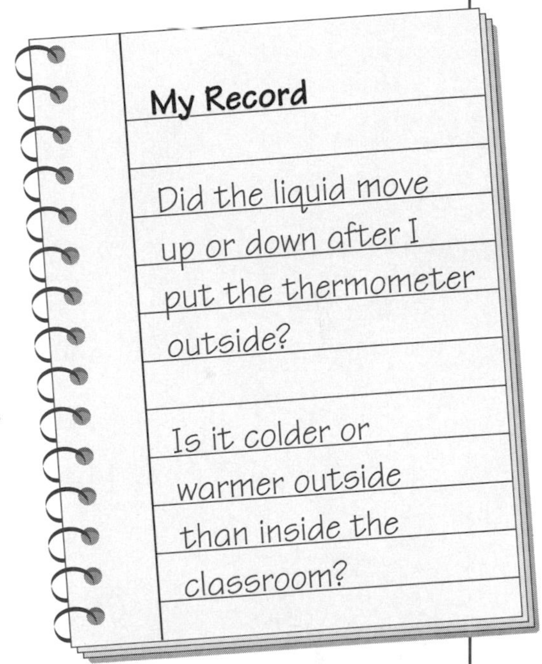

Date	Mon.	Tues.	Wed.	Thurs.	Fri.
Temperature Inside					
Temperature Outside					

Try It Out

Do the experiment on this page for a week. Write the temperature for each day. Does it get colder or warmer or stay the same?

Old MacDonald Had a Farm

Old MacDonald had a farm,
E-I-E-I-O
And on that farm
he had some chicks,
E-I-E-I-O.
With a chick-chick here,
and a chick-chick there,
Here a chick, there a chick,
everywhere a chick-chick.
Old MacDonald had a farm,
E-I-E-I-O.

Make up your own words for "Old MacDonald Had a Farm." Think about all of the animals you can see on a farm. Work in a small group to choose the animals and sounds for your song. Sing your song to the rest of the class.

The Farmer in the Dell

The farmer in the dell,
The farmer in the dell,
Heigh-oh, the derry oh,
The farmer in the dell.

2. The farmer takes a wife.
3. The wife takes a nurse.
4. The nurse takes a child.
5. The child takes a dog.
6. The dog takes a cat.
7. The cat takes a rat.
8. The rat takes the cheese.
9. The cheese stands alone.

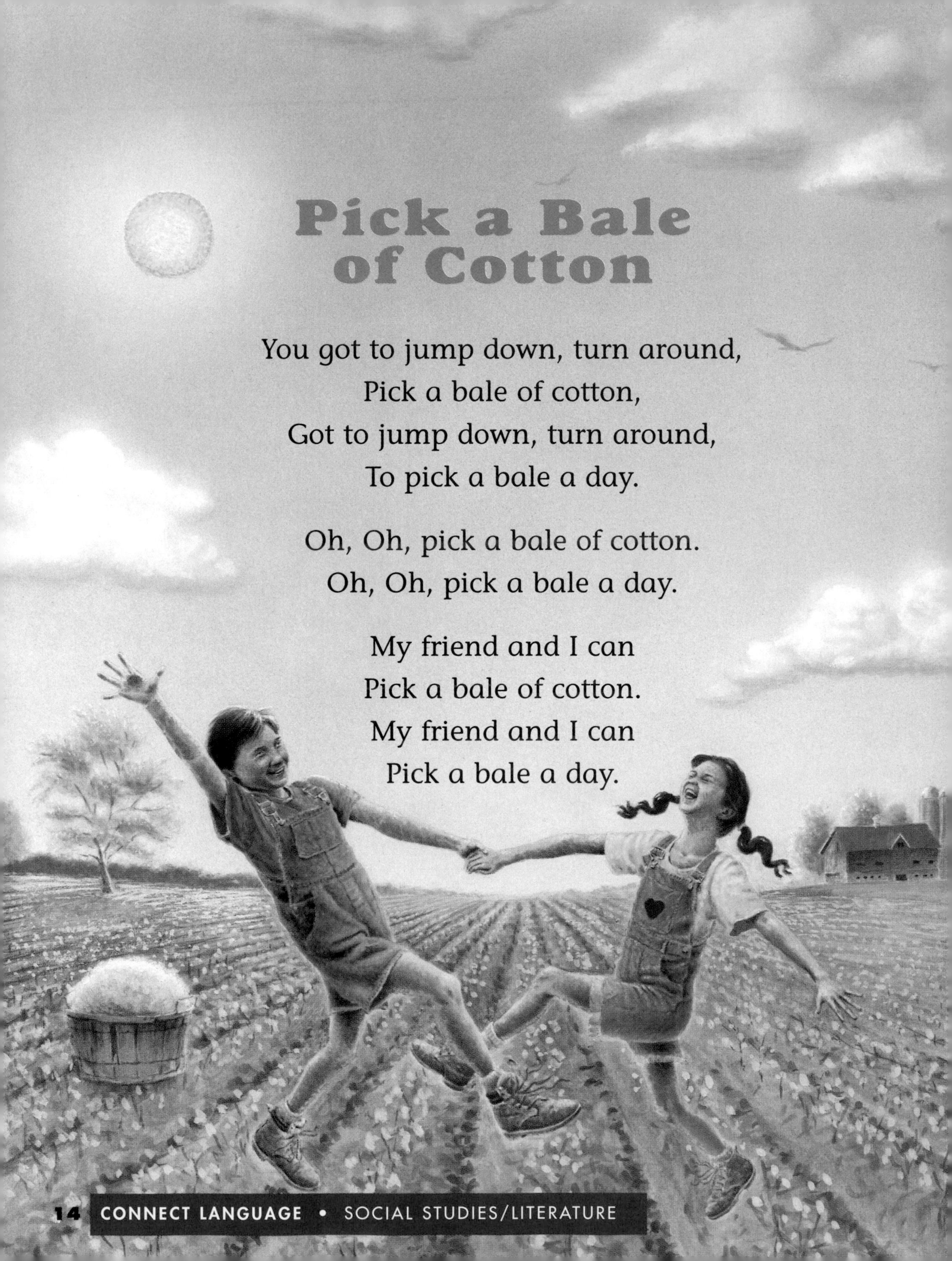

Pick a Bale of Cotton

You got to jump down, turn around,
Pick a bale of cotton,
Got to jump down, turn around,
To pick a bale a day.

Oh, Oh, pick a bale of cotton.
Oh, Oh, pick a bale a day.

My friend and I can
Pick a bale of cotton.
My friend and I can
Pick a bale a day.

Tell what you learned.

CHAPTER 1

1. Draw a picture of a farm. Write about it.

2. Why are farms important to people?

3. Which farm song do you like best? Why?

4. What things did you use or eat yesterday that came from a farm? Make a list. Compare your list with a classmate's.

Life in the City

Tell what you know.

Have you ever been to a big city? Do you live in one now? What do you see in this city?

Word Bank

- office buildings
- people
- restaurants
- stores
- streets
- traffic lights

Talk About It

How is living in a city different from living on a farm? How is it the same?

Where would you most like to live, in a city or in the country? Why?

What is a community?

A **neighborhood** is a place where people live near one another.

A **community** is made up of neighborhoods. A community has homes, stores, schools, restaurants, and movie theaters.

What is your community like?

What is a city?

A city is made up of many communities.

Every city has a **downtown.** The downtown is the part of the city that has many office buildings, shops, and restaurants. It is noisy and busy.

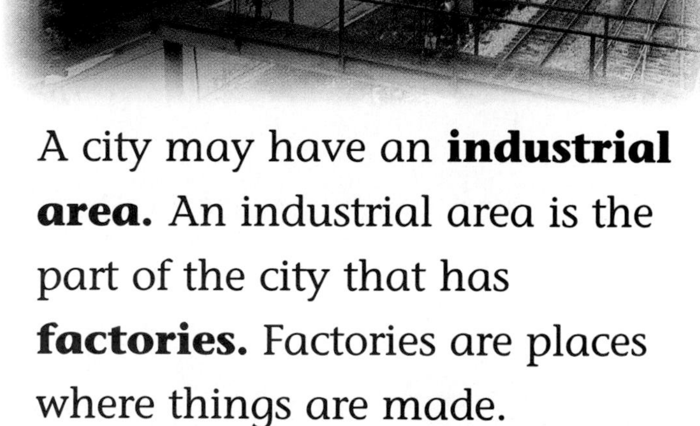

A city may have an **industrial area.** An industrial area is the part of the city that has **factories.** Factories are places where things are made.

Write About It

Make a list of words that describe a city. Which of these words describe where you live?

In Your Community

In your community, you can find many **services** and **goods.** Services are jobs that people do for others. Goods are things people make that you can buy.

▲ You can eat delicious tacos in this neighborhood restaurant.

▲ The police and fire departments keep people safe.

You can buy all kinds of goods for your home at a hardware store.

Taxicab drivers and bus drivers help people get around in the city.

Think About It

Which services and goods in this picture do you and your family use? Which ones are the most important to you?

State Capitals

Some cities are **state capitals**. A state capital is a city where the laws for that state are made. Look at the map. It shows each state's capital.

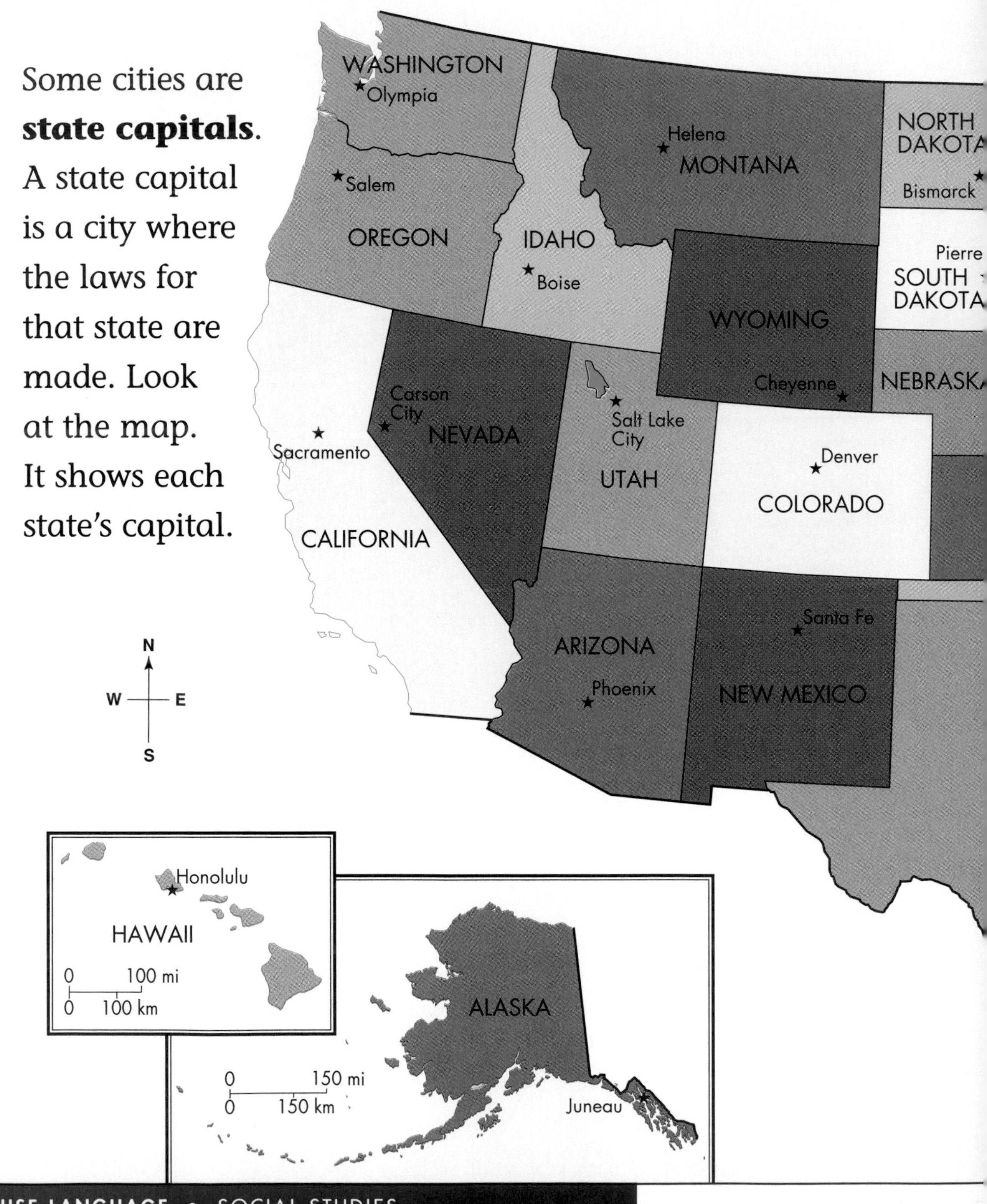

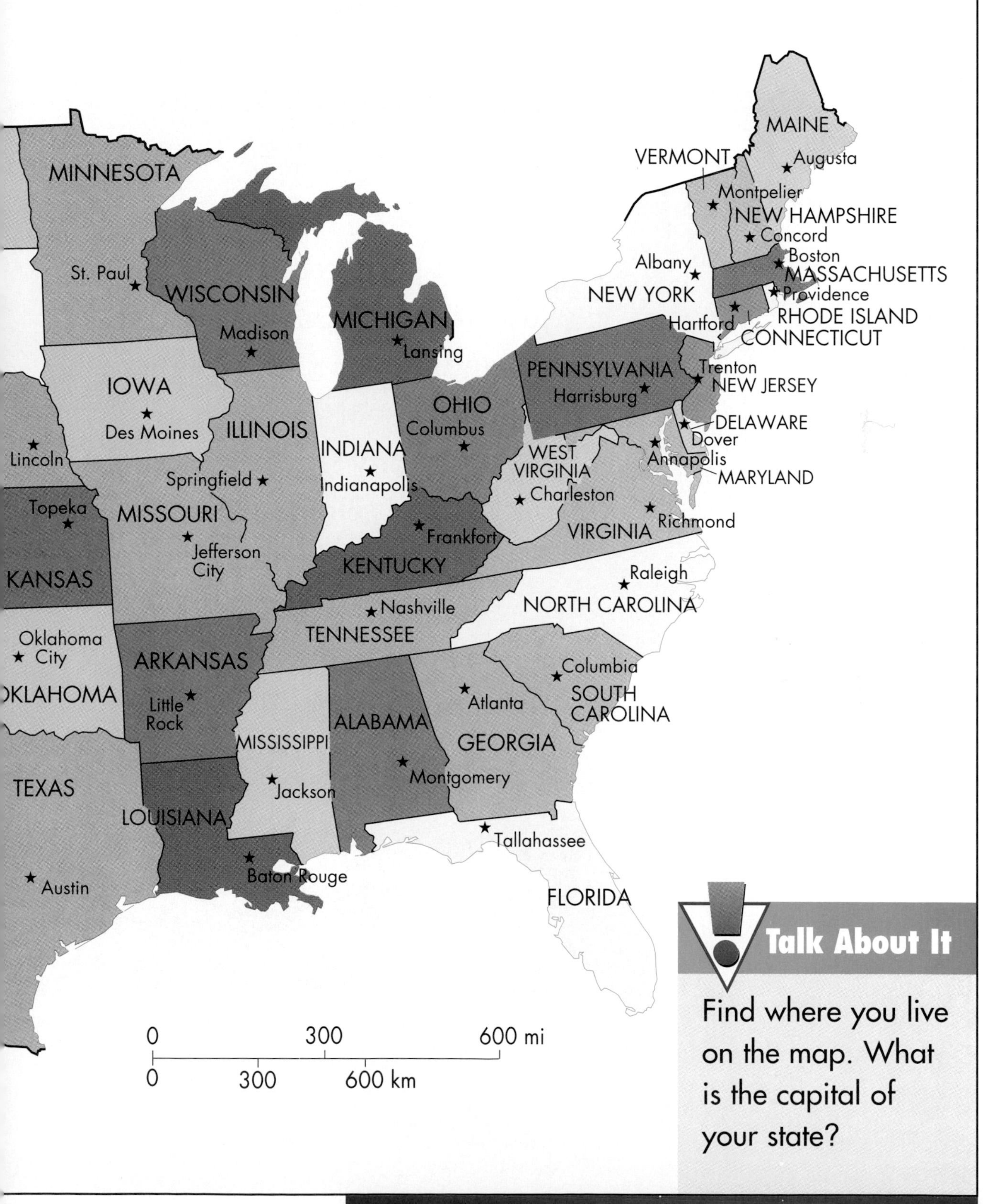

Talk About It

Find where you live on the map. What is the capital of your state?

How much did they eat?

Many cities have food festivals where people can buy different kinds of foods.

There was a food festival in Gloria's city last weekend. On Saturday, the pizza stand sold 465 slices of pizza. On Sunday, it sold 424 slices of pizza. How many slices of pizza did the pizza stand sell in all?

Write About It

Work with a partner to write a food math problem. Give your problem to another pair of friends to solve.

What do you eat?

There are many different kinds of food. Some foods are better for you than other foods. Food can be divided into five groups. If you want to have a healthy diet, every day you should eat food from each food group.

Foods You Need to Eat Every Day

Write About It

You are going to make dinner for your family. Write a shopping list. List one or two foods from each food group.

City Mouse and Country Mouse

a play by Jane Buxton based on Aesop's fable

Reader's Tip
A play is a story that is told by what the characters say. We can read the words of each character and pretend to be that character. This play tells an old story about two mice in a new way.

CHARACTERS

City Mouse (dressed in trendy clothes)
Country Mouse (dressed in overalls and gumboots)
Dog **First Cat** **Second Cat**

SCENE 1

Country Mouse *stands outside a mousehole in the country.* City Mouse *comes in, carrying a suitcase.*

City Mouse Hi there, Country Cousin! Very kind of you to invite me for a holiday. I've never been to the country.

Country Mouse You're welcome, Cousin City Mouse.

City Mouse Is it always so quiet here, Cousin? It's sort of spooky.

Country Mouse Yes, it's peaceful in the country.

City Mouse But what's on in the evenings? Do you go out to a disco? Or do you stay at home and watch TV?

Country Mouse Well, I haven't actually got electricity yet . . .

Language Tip: Vocabulary
A *disco* is a place where people go to dance to music.

City Mouse What?

Country Mouse So I can't watch TV. But I do watch the sun go down. We get some beautiful sunsets here, you know.

City Mouse No TV? No videos?

Country Mouse There is music, though. We have a band called The Cicadas.

City Mouse Cicadas? Never heard of them. Hey, Cousin, I'm hungry. What's for lunch?

Country Mouse Well, I can offer you . . .

Language Tip: Vocabulary
A *cicada* is an insect that makes a loud, sharp sound.

City Mouse You haven't got any pizzas, have you? Back home I hang out in a pizza parlor. I can really pig out there. Believe me, Cousin, a pizza parlor's a cool spot for a mouse.

Country Mouse I'm afraid I don't have anything like that. But here's a freshly picked ear of wheat and some acorns. If you're still hungry, I can get you some fine windfall apples.

City Mouse Sorry, I'm not really into health foods. Look, this holiday isn't going to work out. I suppose tonight you'll expect me to watch a good old-fashioned sunset with you.

Country Mouse Well . . . I . . . er . . .

City Mouse I thought as much. I don't want to be rude, Cousin, but don't you think it's a little *boring* here?

Language Tip: Vocabulary
Pig out means "to eat a lot."

Strategy Tip: Stop and Think
City Mouse and Country Mouse find out that the city and the country are different. How are they different so far?

Strategy Tip:
Step into the Story
Be City Mouse. How do you feel about the country?

Reader's Tip
Do not read aloud the words inside the ( ). These words tell the actors what to do.

Country Mouse Is it? Well, perhaps it is . . . I've never thought about it. What's it like in the city?

City Mouse It's cool, mouse. There's always something on in the city. But the best thing is the food—pizzas, crisps, fizzy drink, ice cream . . .

Country Mouse It sounds too good to be true.

City Mouse Well, it's not too late. We could go now.

Country Mouse Now? To the city?

City Mouse Sure. Why not? I don't think I could spend the night here. It's so quiet I wouldn't get to sleep.

Country Mouse All right I *will* go to the city with you. I'd certainly like to try some of that delicious food.

City Mouse Cool, mouse! Let's go!
(They both leave.)

Reader's Tip
This is a new scene. City Mouse and Country Mouse are now in a new place. Where are they?

SCENE 2

Outside a mousehole under a table in the city. Loud music. Flashing lights. City Mouse *pulls up an empty cigarette packet for* Country Mouse *to sit on. Music fades.*

City Mouse Have a seat, Cousin.

Country Mouse Thank you. Nice place you have here. Will it be dinner time soon?

City Mouse Sure will. This is called a birthday party.
(A large human foot descends beside them.)
Watch out!

Country Mouse *(jumping up)* Yikes! What's that?
(The foot moves away.)

City Mouse That was a human foot. Have to watch out for them. Here's some food dropping now. Crackers and cheese. Help yourself. Be my guest.

Country Mouse Why, thank you, Cousin. It looks delicious.

(Enter Dog.)

Dog Woof, woof, woof!

Language Tip: Vocabulary
Trembling means "shaking." *Shrugging* means "lifting the shoulders as if he doesn't care." Act out the words *trembling* and *shrugging*.

City Mouse Quick! Quick! Into the hole.
(Both Mice run into the hole and peep out as the dog runs off.)

Country Mouse *(trembling)* My, that was close.

City Mouse *(shrugging)* You get used to it.
(Both Mice come out and sit under the table again. Some salami drops from the table. City Mouse *picks it up and gives it to* Country Mouse.*)*

City Mouse Have some salami. Now this is *real* food. Beats acorns any day, don't you think?

Country Mouse What's it made of?

City Mouse Cats!

(He runs into the mousehole.)

Country Mouse *(looking at the salami in horror)* Cats?

(He drops the salami.)

City Mouse No, you nerd. The cats are coming!

(He reaches out and pulls Country Mouse *into the hole just as the cats enter.)*

First Cat Meow. I smell mice.

Second Cat Meyum, yum. I smell salami.

(Cats *share salami and leave.* City Mouse *comes out of the hole, dragging* Country Mouse *behind him.)*

City Mouse Drat those cats. They've eaten our salami.

Country Mouse *(trembling)* At least they haven't eaten us.

Strategy Tip: Stop and Think
Why does Country Mouse drop the salami? What does he think the salami is made of?

Strategy Tip: Step into the Story
Be Country Mouse. How do you feel about the city? Do you think you will stay in the city?

City Mouse Don't be a wimp, Cousin Country Mouse. Live dangerously. Have some fun while you're in the city. Ah, look! There's a spilt glass of something or other.

Country Mouse Ooh, I've never tasted Something or Other before.

(Both Mice creep closer. A human hand reaches out for the glass.)

City Mouse Run for it!

Country Mouse Help!

(They run to the mousehole. Music begins—the Happy Birthday song.)

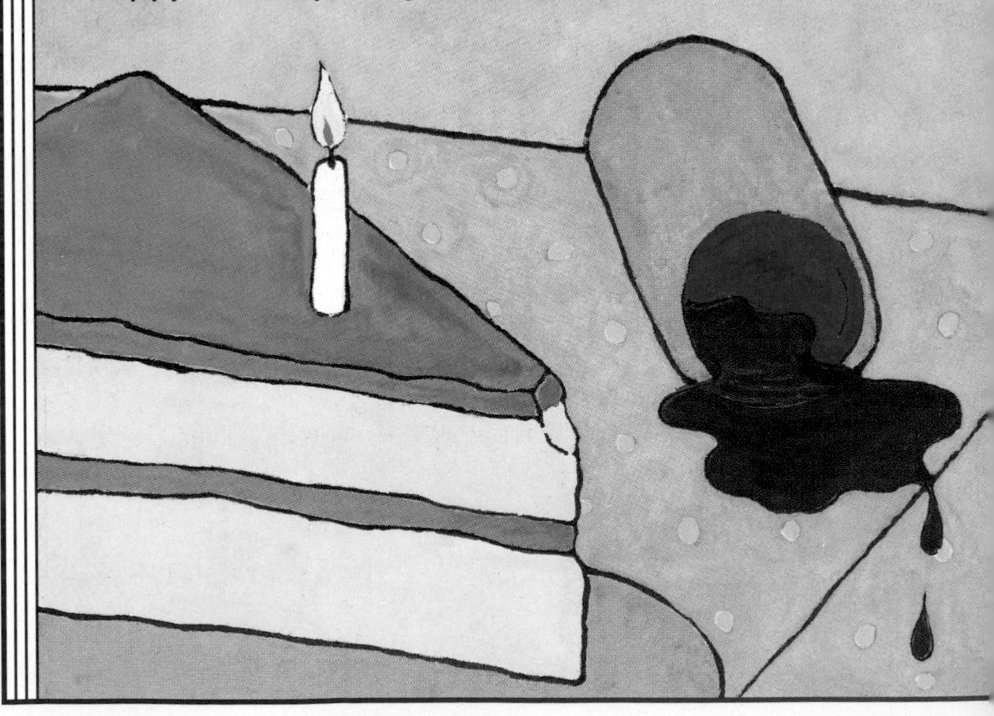

City Mouse Cool, mouse, cool! They're playing the cake music. Wait till you taste the cake! And icing! And candles! Delicious!

Country Mouse I'll take your word for it, Cousin City Mouse. But I'm not staying for the cake.

City Mouse You won't stay?

Country Mouse No. I've just remembered something I have to do back home. Goodbye and thank you.

City Mouse Well, goodbye, Cousin. I hope you enjoyed city life. But what have you suddenly remembered?

Country Mouse I've remembered how I can take off my boots and relax when I'm in the country. If I hurry home, I'll be just in time to sit by my front door and watch the sunset. Goodbye!

Reader's Tip
What lesson does this story teach? Where is each mouse happy?

Sing a Song of Cities

by Lee Bennett Hopkins

Sing a song of cities.
If you do,
Cities will sing back to you.

They'll sing in subway roars and rumbles.
People-laughs, machine-loud-grumbles.

Sing a song of cities.
If you do,
Cities will sing back to you.

Tell what you learned.

CHAPTER 2

1. Draw pictures of people and places that provide goods and services in a city. Write about your pictures. Share your work with classmates.

2. Make one shopping list for Country Mouse and one for City Mouse. How many things do they buy that are the same?

3. Make a chart of the five food groups. Look on page 25 for help. Write the name of a food you like from each food group.

4. What did you most enjoy learning about life in the city?

CHAPTER 3

How You Use Light

Tell what you know.

What kinds of light do you use?

Word Bank

- candlelight
- electric light
- flashlight
- street light
- sunlight

Talk About It

When do you use different kinds of light?

Light: Long Ago and Today

Long ago, people used **fire** to light their caves.

In the past, sailors on ships used light from the **stars** to help them find their way.

In the 1870s, some people used light from **gas lamps** to light their homes. Other people used **oil lamps** or **candles.**

Today, people use **electric lights** to light their homes, stores, factories, offices, and many other places.

Think About It

Name all the kinds of lights you use in a week.

A Time Line of Lights

Thomas Edison invented the electric light bulb in 1879. What lights were invented before the light bulb? What lights were invented after the light bulb? Look at the time line to find out.

1815

Sir Humphry Davy invented the miner's safety lamp for use in mines.

1816

Thomas Drummond invented the limelight. It was used to light theaters.

1879

Thomas Edison invented the electric light bulb.

Use the time line to answer these questions.

In what year was the electric traffic light invented?

Which was invented first, the neon light or the limelight?

Which was invented first, the miner's safety lamp or the laser?

What happened in the year 1879?

Write About It

Make a time line of your life. List three or four important events in your life.

1910

Georges Claude invented the neon light.

1923

Garrett Morgan invented the electric traffic light.

1960

Theodore Harold Maiman invented the laser for use in science and medicine.

Lights Where You Live

Lights help your **community** in many ways. What kinds of lights do you see?

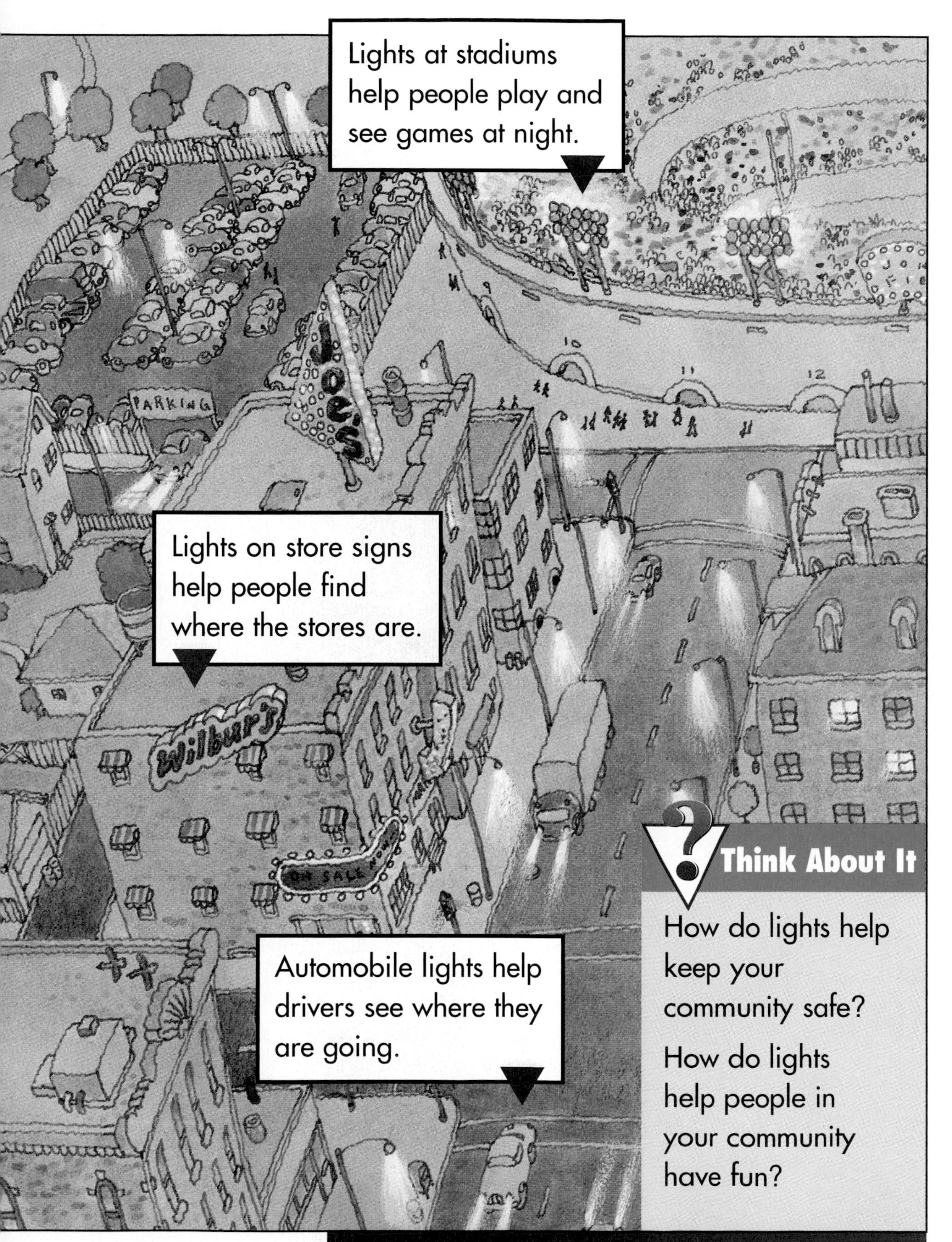

Lights at stadiums help people play and see games at night.

Lights on store signs help people find where the stores are.

Automobile lights help drivers see where they are going.

Think About It

How do lights help keep your community safe?

How do lights help people in your community have fun?

How do you see?

You use your eyes to see.

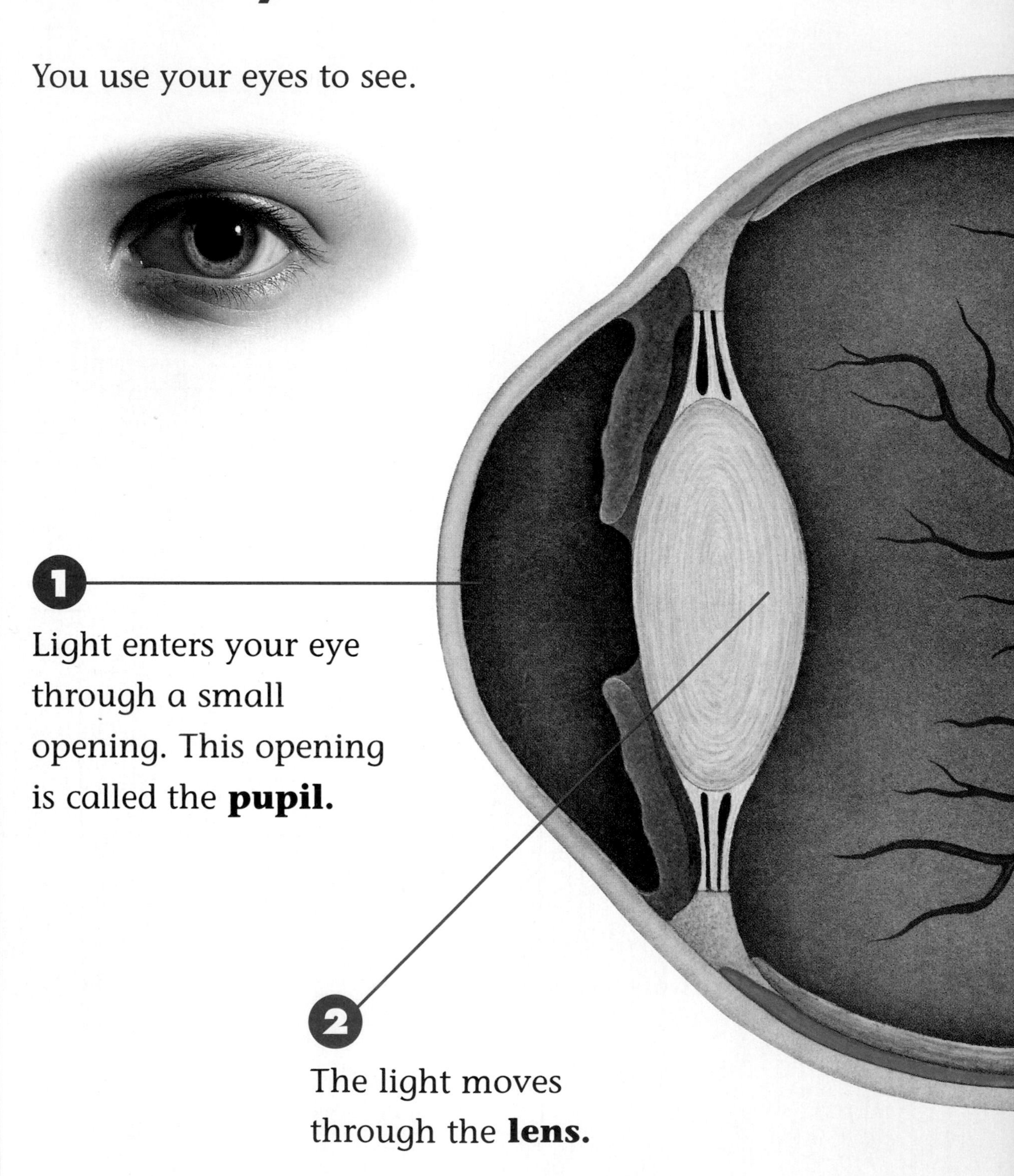

1 Light enters your eye through a small opening. This opening is called the **pupil.**

2 The light moves through the **lens.**

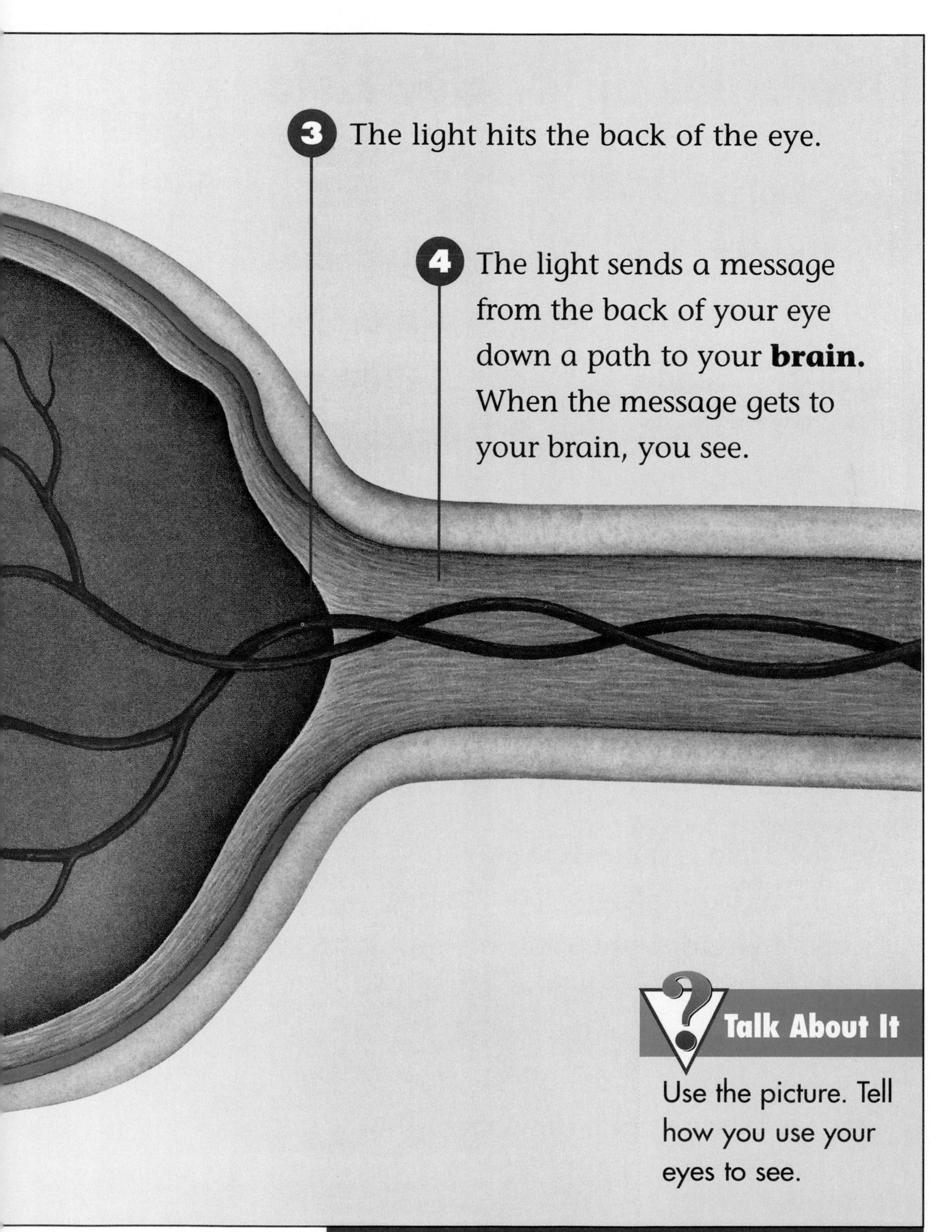

3 The light hits the back of the eye.

4 The light sends a message from the back of your eye down a path to your **brain.** When the message gets to your brain, you see.

Talk About It

Use the picture. Tell how you use your eyes to see.

The Lights of Wrigley Field

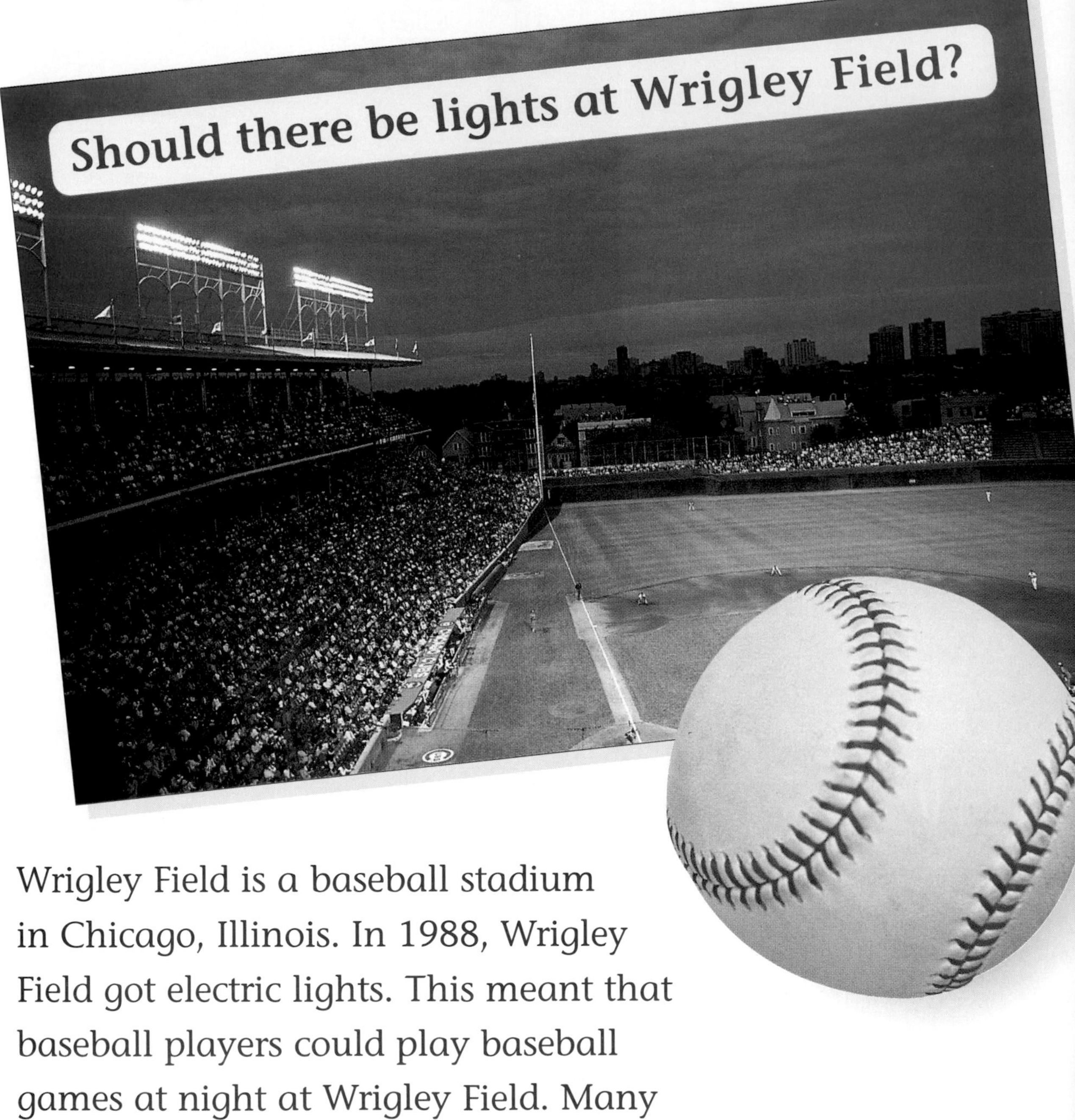

Wrigley Field is a baseball stadium in Chicago, Illinois. In 1988, Wrigley Field got electric lights. This meant that baseball players could play baseball games at night at Wrigley Field. Many fans were happy about the change. Other fans were not happy about the change. Two fans wrote to the mayor.

Dear Mr. Mayor:

I like baseball. On warm summer nights, my parents take me to Wrigley Field to see the games. I can't go to afternoon games because my parents work during the day. The only time we can see the games together is at night. Please don't ever turn the lights off at night.

A baseball fan,
Paco Martínez

Write About It

Make two lists. In one list, write what is good about having the lights on at Wrigley Field. In the other list, write what is not good. Which side do you agree with?

Dear Mr. Mayor:

My father and I often go to Wrigley Field to watch baseball games. We always go in the afternoon. I don't like night games because we live close to Wrigley Field. The lights keep me awake. The traffic, people, and noise keep me awake too. So please turn the lights off at Wrigley Field.

Your friend,
Erica Baker

The Park

by James S. Tippett

I'm glad that I
Live near a park
For in the winter
After dark
The park lights shine
As bright and still
As dandelions
On a hill.

Tell what you learned.

CHAPTER 3

1. Draw a picture of the parts of your eye that help you see. Look at the picture of the eye on pages 48 and 49 for help. Label the parts. Use your drawing to tell a friend how you see.

2. List two ways that light helps your community.

3. Imagine that you live near Wrigley Field. Write a letter telling how you feel about the lights.

4. What did you learn about light that you didn't know before?

What Light Can Do

Tell what you know.

What does each picture tell about light?

Talk About It

What do you see when you look through a window?

What do you see when you look in a mirror?

What can light move through?

Light can move through some things. Light can move through **glass.**

▼

Light cannot move through some things. Light cannot move through a wall.

▼ 

Sometimes when light ▶ moves, it **bends.** Light bends when it moves from water to air.

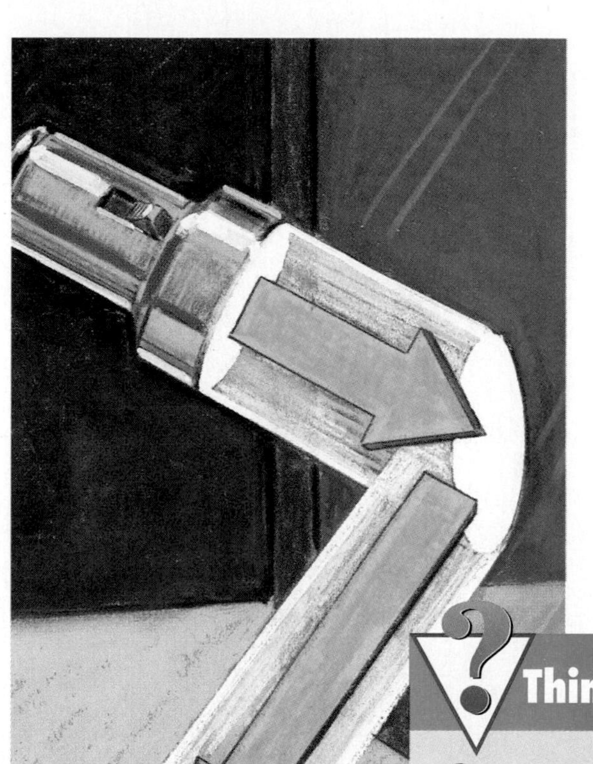

◀ When light hits smooth, shiny things, the light **bounces back**. Light bounces back when it hits a mirror.

Think About It

Can you see through a book? Why or why not?

Can you see through a mirror? Why or why not?

Make light bounce.

Things You Need

 foil square
 cardboard square
 clear plastic square
 tape
flashlight

Follow these steps.

1. Put the foil square on top of the cardboard square. Make sure the shiny side faces up.
2. Cover the foil with the plastic square. Tape the squares together. Now you have a mirror.

3. Shine the flashlight on your mirror.

4. Move the mirror. See what happens to the light.

Think About It

What happens to the light when it shines on the mirror? Why does this happen?

What do you think will happen to the light if you shine it on a cardboard square? Why?

Make a rainbow.

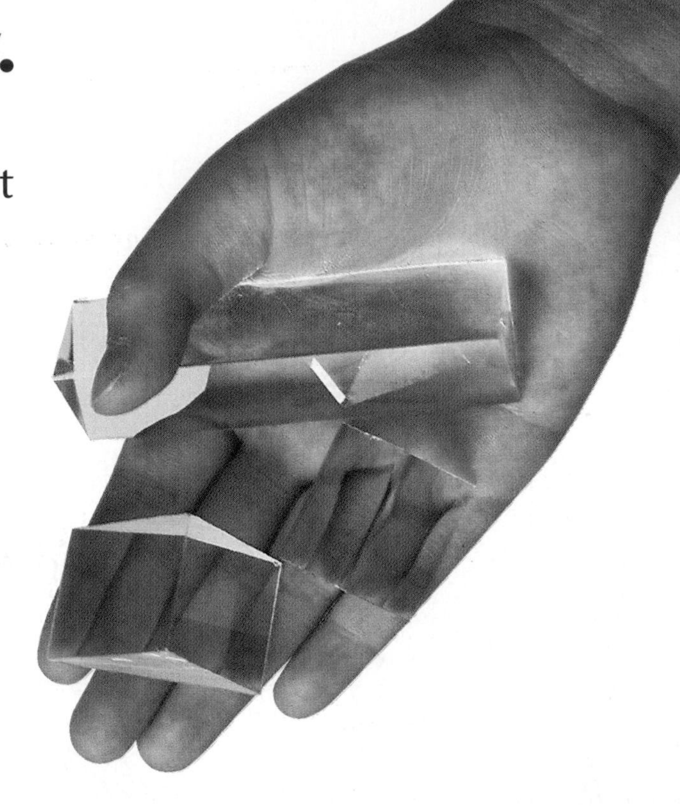

Light is made up of different colors. When light moves through a **prism,** you can see these colors. A prism separates light into the colors of the rainbow.

Things You Need

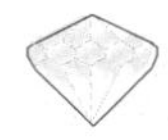 prism

 bright sunny day

 white paper

Follow these steps.

1. Hold the white paper in sunlight.

2. Hold the prism between the sunlight and the white paper.

3. Move the prism. Look for the rainbow colors on the paper.

Word Bank

- blue
- green
- orange
- red
- violet
- yellow

My Record

What happened when light moved through the prism?

Write About It

Draw your own picture of a rainbow. Label each color on your rainbow.

A Shadow Play

Light cannot move through your hands. A **shadow** forms where the light cannot go.

You can put on a play with shadows. In Indonesia, **shadow plays** are very popular. Sometimes the plays last all night.

Make your own shadow puppet. Then work with a friend to make your own shadow play.

Things You Need

 paper

 crayons

 scissors

 tape

 craft stick

 flashlight

Follow these steps.

1. Draw an animal on the paper. Cut out the animal. Then tape the animal to a craft stick.
2. Shine the flashlight on a wall. Hold the puppet close to the light from the flashlight. Look at the shadow on the wall.
3. Work with your friend. Make up a shadow play with the two puppets.

Think About It

What happens if you move the puppet farther away from the flashlight?

Why does this happen?

Singing Birds and Flashing Fireflies

by Dorothy Hinshaw Patent

illustrated by Mary Morgan

Strategy Tip:
Use What You Know
In this picture, the children are waving and smiling. The picture helps you better understand the meaning of *communicate.*

People talk to each other every day. When you tell a friend to meet you at the playground after school, your friend understands and joins you there. Animals, too, need ways to tell each other things, or *communicate* (Kah-mew-nih-kate).

There are different ways of communicating. People don't just use their voices. They also show how they feel with a smile, a frown, a friendly pat on the back, or a kiss. Like people, animals need to "talk" to one another. But animals don't have words. So how do they communicate?

Language Tip: Contractions
Don't combines the two words, *do* and *not.*

Special Ways of Communicating

Dogs bark or growl. Horses neigh. Male crickets rub their wings together to make the chirping sounds that attract females. Some fish grate their teeth together to make sounds.

Many animals use their tails to show how they feel. Some crabs and spiders wave their legs in special patterns to attract a mate.

Dogs, horses, and cats use their ears not only to hear but also to show how they are feeling. They flatten them back if they are angry or let them stand straight up if they are alert, eager, or happy.

Singing Birds

Have you ever heard the lovely song of a sparrow in the morning? When birds sing, they are not using real language the way humans do. While humans can speak hundreds of different languages, each kind of bird has only one "language" with a few "words."

Language Tip: Stop and Think
What is the difference between "bird language" and "human language"?

We can tell each other all kinds of things with words. But birds have only a few messages they can get across. A person can say the same thing in different ways. "Please come to my birthday party on Saturday" means the same as "Saturday is my birthday. Can you come to my party?" But a bird has only one way of saying "This is my place."

Language Tip: Idioms
Get across means "to communicate."

Flashing Fireflies

Many animals depend more on sight than sound to get messages across. The sparkling flashes of fireflies across a nighttime meadow are beautiful to us. But they provide important information to the fireflies.

Strategy Tip: Use Pictures for Meaning
What is the firefly doing on the top of the plant? How does this help you understand what *perch* means?

Female fireflies often perch on the tops of plants, while the males fly above them, flashing bright signals.

There are many kinds of fireflies, and each kind has its own special flashing code. When a female sees the proper code, she waits just the right amount of time. Then she flashes back.

Language Tip: Use Clues from the Sentence
Heads means "to move to" and *lands* means "to come to a stop at a place."

When a male sees a flash from the grass at the right time, he turns and heads to the spot. Here is a female of his kind. As he approaches, he flashes again and she answers. When he gets close, he lands on the grass and walks toward her, flashing as he comes.

Ways of "Talking"

You can see that animals communicate in many ways. They use sight, sound, smell, and touch. Next time you go for a walk in the park or to the zoo, see if you can figure out how the animals you see are "talking" to each other.

Reader's Tip
Often, the end of a reading *summarizes.* It tells you what the main idea of the reading is. What was this reading about?

Lightning Bugs

by Ericka Northrop

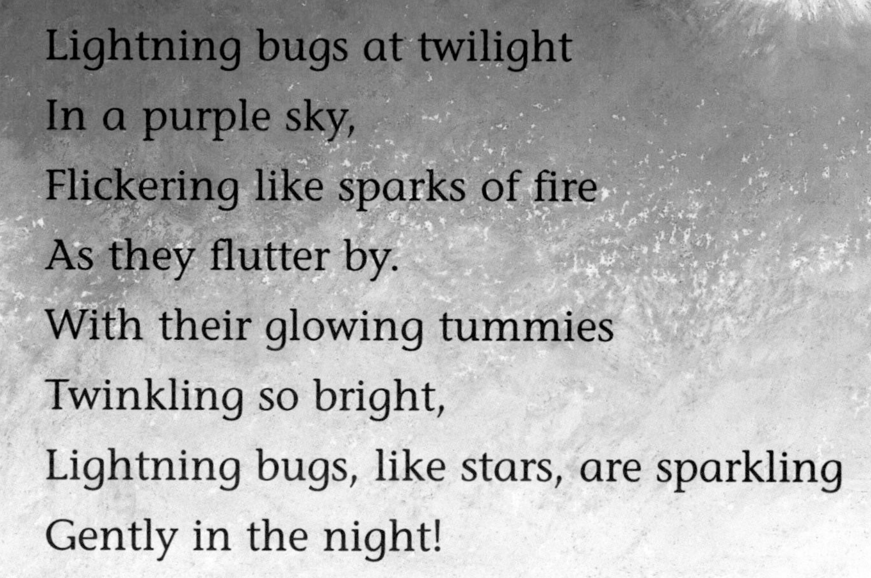

Lightning bugs at twilight
In a purple sky,
Flickering like sparks of fire
As they flutter by.
With their glowing tummies
Twinkling so bright,
Lightning bugs, like stars, are sparkling
Gently in the night!

Try It Out

Use a flashlight to communicate like lightning bugs. Decide with a partner what one flash means and what two flashes mean.

Tell what you learned.

1. Work with a friend. Make a chart like this one and complete it.

Things that light can move through	Things that light cannot move through

2. What happens when light moves from water to air?

3. Draw a picture of two animals communicating with each other. Write what the animals are saying.

4. What was the most interesting thing you learned about light? What else would you like to know about light?

CHAPTER 5

How You Make Sound

Tell what you know.

What is sound?

Look at the picture. Who or what is making sound?

Word Bank

- fireworks
- music
- musicians
- people
- clapping
- exploding
- talking

Talk About It

What are some of the sounds you hear where you live?

Which sounds do you like?

How is sound made?

Sounds may seem different. But they are all alike in one way. All sounds are a form of **energy**. Energy is the power to work or act. Other examples of energy are light, heat, and electricity.

1. When an object moves back and forth quickly, it **vibrates.**
2. The **vibrations** make **sound waves**. Sound waves are a form of energy that you can hear.

3 The sound waves travel through the air. They enter your ears. Your brain tells you what you hear.

Think About It

What is a vibration?

What are some things in your classroom that make sound waves?

Make a ruler sing.

You can't see sound waves. But sometimes you can see objects vibrate. You can feel the vibrations. You can hear the vibrations.

Try this experiment.

Things You Need

- thin ruler
- desk or table

Follow these steps.

1. Hold the ruler on the side of the desk.

2. Push the tip of the ruler down. Then let it go. What do you see? What do you hear?

3. Move the ruler so that more of it is on the desk.

4. Repeat step 2.

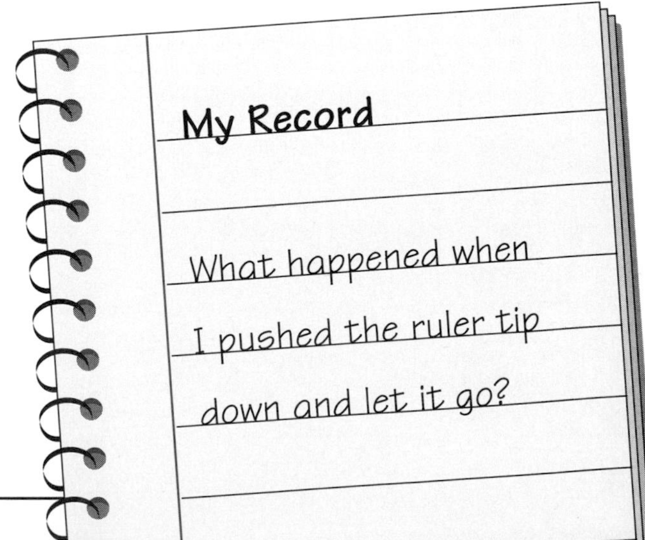

How did the sound change when you moved the ruler?

Why do you think this happened?

How Sounds Are Different

Sounds can be loud. Sounds can be soft. **Volume** is how loud or how soft a sound is.

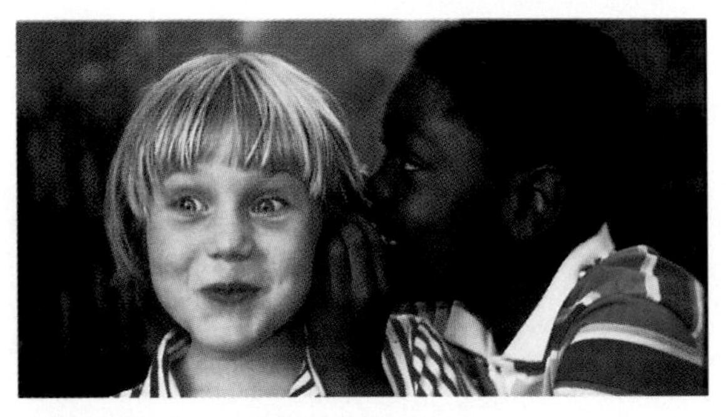

▲ A whisper is a soft sound.

▲ A jet plane makes a loud sound.

Make a chart. Tell about the volume of each sound. Add some of your own sounds. Write *loud* or *soft*.

Volume	
a fire-truck siren	
a small bell ringing	
blowing leaves	
a drummer playing	

Sounds can be high. Sounds can be low. **Pitch** is how high or how low a sound is.

▲ A kitten makes a high-pitched sound.

▲ A lion makes a low-pitched sound.

Make a chart. Tell about the pitch of each sound. Add some of your own sounds. Write *high* or *low*.

Think About It

What loud sound can you make?

What high sound can you make?

Music, Music Everywhere!

Music is everywhere. You can hear different musical instruments all over the world.

The **sansa** is from Africa. To play it, push the metal sticks with your thumbs. ▼

The **cabaca** is from South America. To play it, hold the stick and turn the beads. ▼

The **Guatemalan pan pipe** is from Guatemala. To play it, blow into it. ▼

◀ The **shakuhachi** is from Japan. It is made from bamboo. To play it, blow into it.

Write About It

Draw a picture of a musical instrument from your family's country. Write the name of the instrument on the picture. Write about how you play it. Show and tell about your picture to your classmates.

Minnie the Mambo Mosquito

by Carmen Tafolla

illustrated by Ruben Ramos

Language Tip: Vocabulary
Mosquito is the same word in English and in Spanish. It means "little fly."

Minnie the Mosquito *loved* to dance!

She danced the mambo and the bamba,
And the Cotton-eyed Joe!
She danced the cumbia and the samba
And the waltz just so!
She danced the Mexican polka
And the twist while she flew!
She danced the boogie-woogie
And the hokey-pokey, too!

Minnie traveled far and wide to find music—but whenever she found it, and started dancing, someone would turn off the radio and say, "I hear mosquitoes. Let's go inside."

Or the band would stop playing and say, "There are too many bugs out here. Let's go home."

Or the choir would stop singing and say, "Let's go inside before the mosquitoes start biting."

When that happened, Minnie would buzz, "Wait a minute! I'm not like those other mosquitoes that bite! I just like to dance!" But they never heard her.

Language Tip: Vocabulary
Flying stunts are tricks in the air.

All of her mosquito friends would practice their flying stunts.

They would practice dive-bombing.

Vrrr-rrr-RRRR-RRROOOM!

They would practice biting.

Strategy Tip:
Stop and Think
How is Minnie different from her friends?

But Minnie just practiced dancing—every time she heard music.

She danced the mambo and the bamba,
And the Cotton-eyed Joe!
She danced the cumbia and the samba
And the waltz just so!
She danced the Mexican polka
And the twist while she flew!
She danced the boogie-woogie
And the hokey-pokey, too!

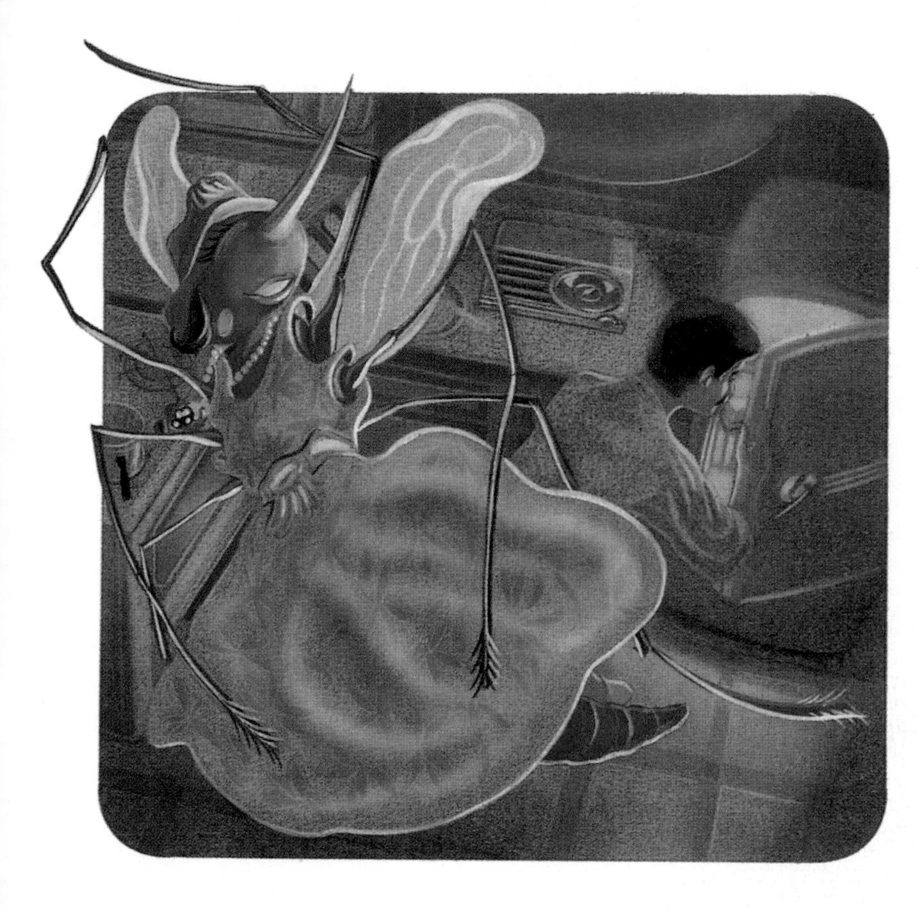

One day, Minnie found Fred.

Fred loved music almost as much as Minnie loved dancing. He liked to play his radio in the morning. He liked to play his radio in the afternoon. He even liked to play his radio all night long! Fred *never* turned his radio off.

Minnie liked Fred.

Strategy Tip: Stop and Think
What does Fred do that Minnie likes?

When Fred's radio played a waltz, Minnie waltzed while Fred sang "La—la—la—la la! La la! La la!" When Fred's radio played a Mexican polka, Minnie danced the Mexican polka while Fred shouted, "*¡A-jai!*" When Fred's radio played the Cotton-eyed Joe, Minnie danced the Cotton-eyed Joe while Fred said, "Aw-haw!"

While all the other mosquitoes were practicing their flying stunts,

and their dive-bombing,

Vrrr-RRR-RRRRROOM

and their biting,

ping

OUCH!

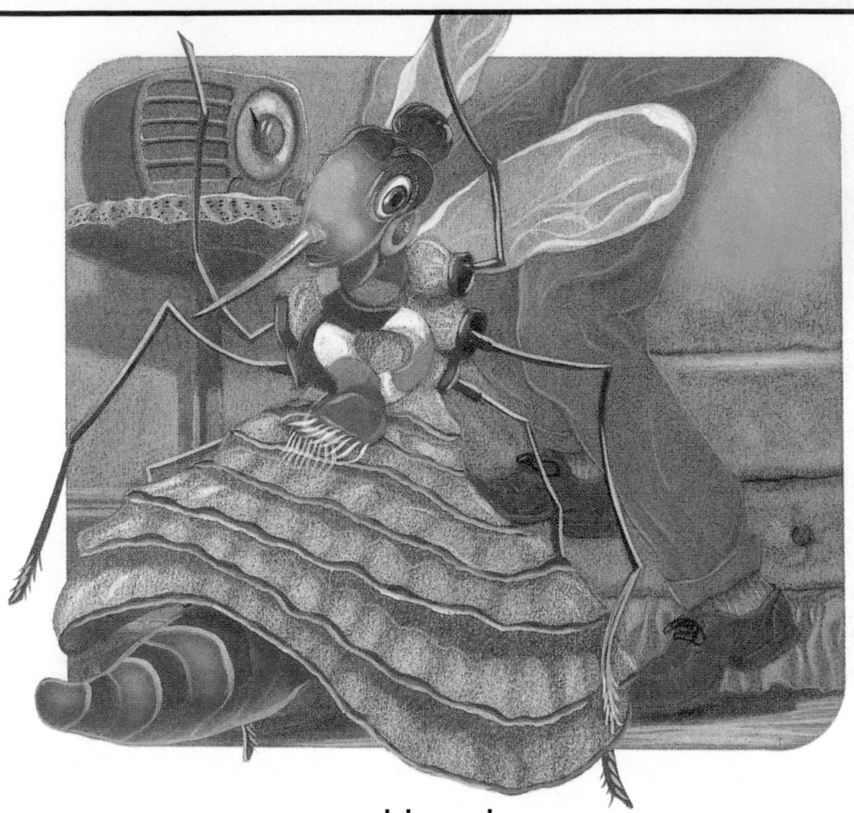

Minnie just practiced her dancing.

She danced the mambo and the bamba,
And the Cotton-eyed Joe!
She danced the cumbia and the samba
And the waltz just so!
She danced the Mexican polka
And the twist while she flew!
She danced the boogie-woogie
And the hokey-pokey, too!

And she never bit Fred at all.

But one day, Fred turned off the radio.

Minnie couldn't believe it! For the first time in her life, she went

Strategy Tip: Making Predictions
Making a prediction helps you understand the story. What do you think Minnie will do next?

But at the very last minute, Minnie took a good look at Fred. She thought about all the good times they had together. She thought about their waltzes, and their polkas, and their Cotton-eyed Joes. . .

and Minnie flew up to Fred's ear and said, "Bz—Bz—Bz—buzz buzz! Buzz buzz! Buzz buzz!"

Something about that buzzing sound made Fred think of music again. Fred turned the radio back on.

And as for Minnie—

She danced the mambo and the bamba,
And the Cotton-eyed Joe!
She danced the cumbia and the samba
And the waltz just so!
She danced the Mexican polka
And the twist while she flew!
She danced the boogie-woogie
And the hokey-pokey, too!

Ears Hear

by Lucia and James L. Hymes, Jr.

Flies buzz,
Motors roar.
Kettles hiss,
People snore.
Dogs bark,
Birds cheep.
Autos honk: *Beep! Beep!*

Winds sigh,
Shoes squeak.
Trucks honk,
Floors creak.
Whistles toot,
Bells clang.
Doors slam: *Bang! Bang!*

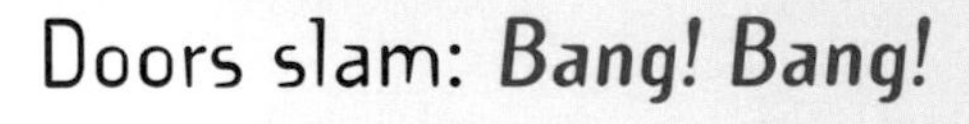

Kids shout,
Clocks ding.
Babies cry,
Phones ring.
Balls bounce,
Spoons drop.
People scream: *Stop! Stop!*

Tell what you learned.

1. How are sounds different?

2. Minnie the Mambo Mosquito loved to dance. What activities with music do you enjoy? Draw a picture of yourself doing a favorite activity. Show your picture to your classmates. Ask them to guess what you are doing.

3. You hear many kinds of sounds. Which ones are most important to you? Why?

4. Make a chart like the one below. Think about some sounds that you heard today. Tell about each sound. Was it loud or soft? Was it high or low?

Sound	Volume	Pitch

How You Use Sound

Tell what you know.

Look at the pictures.

What sounds are these living things making?

Word Bank

- barking
- buzzing
- crying
- hissing
- rattling
- singing
- talking

Talk About It

Make the sounds of the living things shown on these pages.

Why do people and animals make sounds?

How You Hear Sound

You hear sound because sound waves travel through your ears.

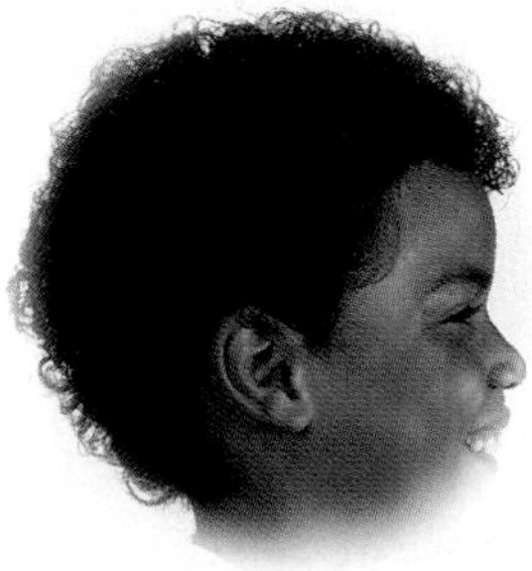

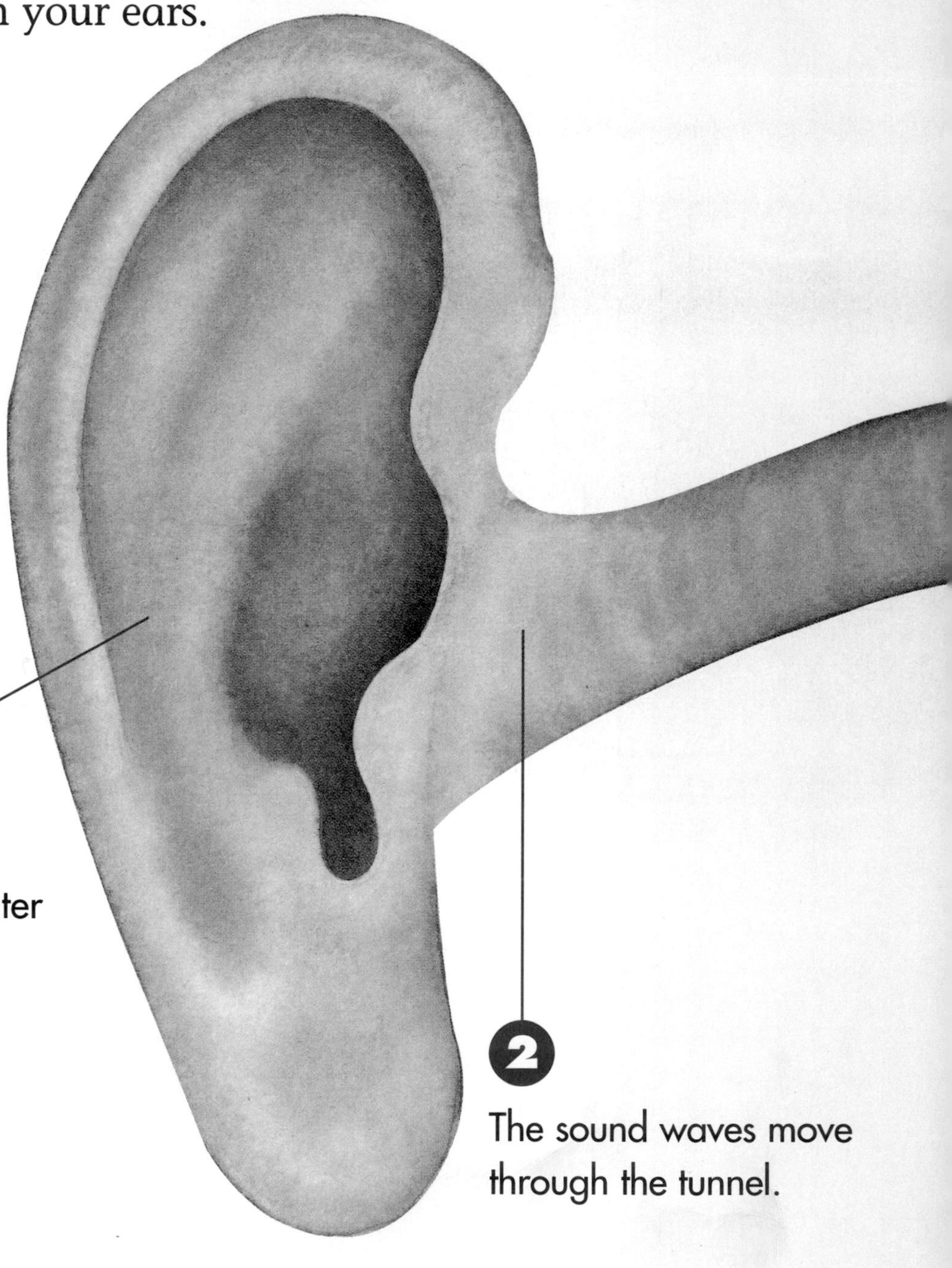

Sound waves enter the outer ear.

The sound waves move through the tunnel.

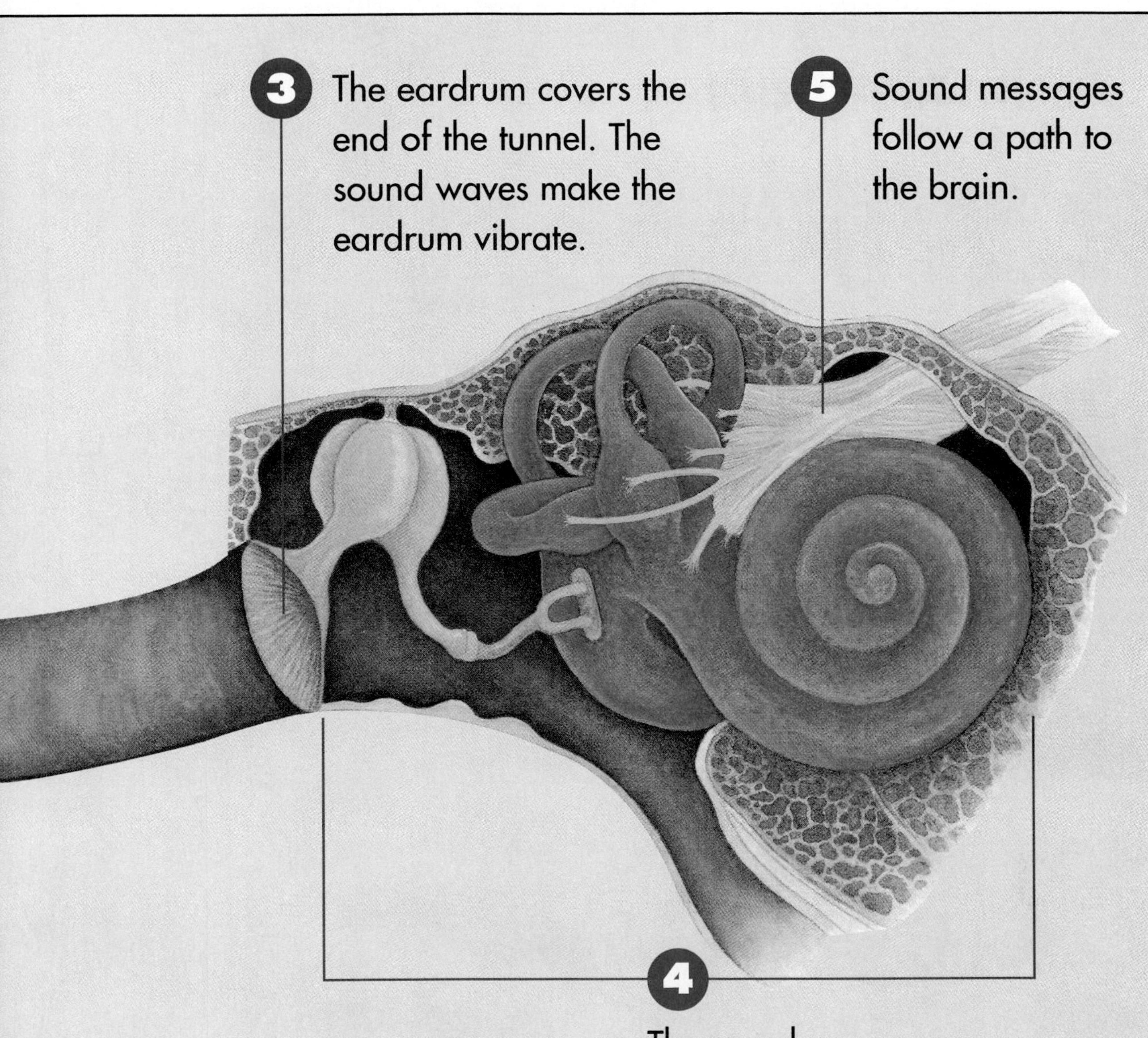

Use the picture. Tell a classmate how you hear sound.

Animals' Ears

Ears help animals survive in many ways.

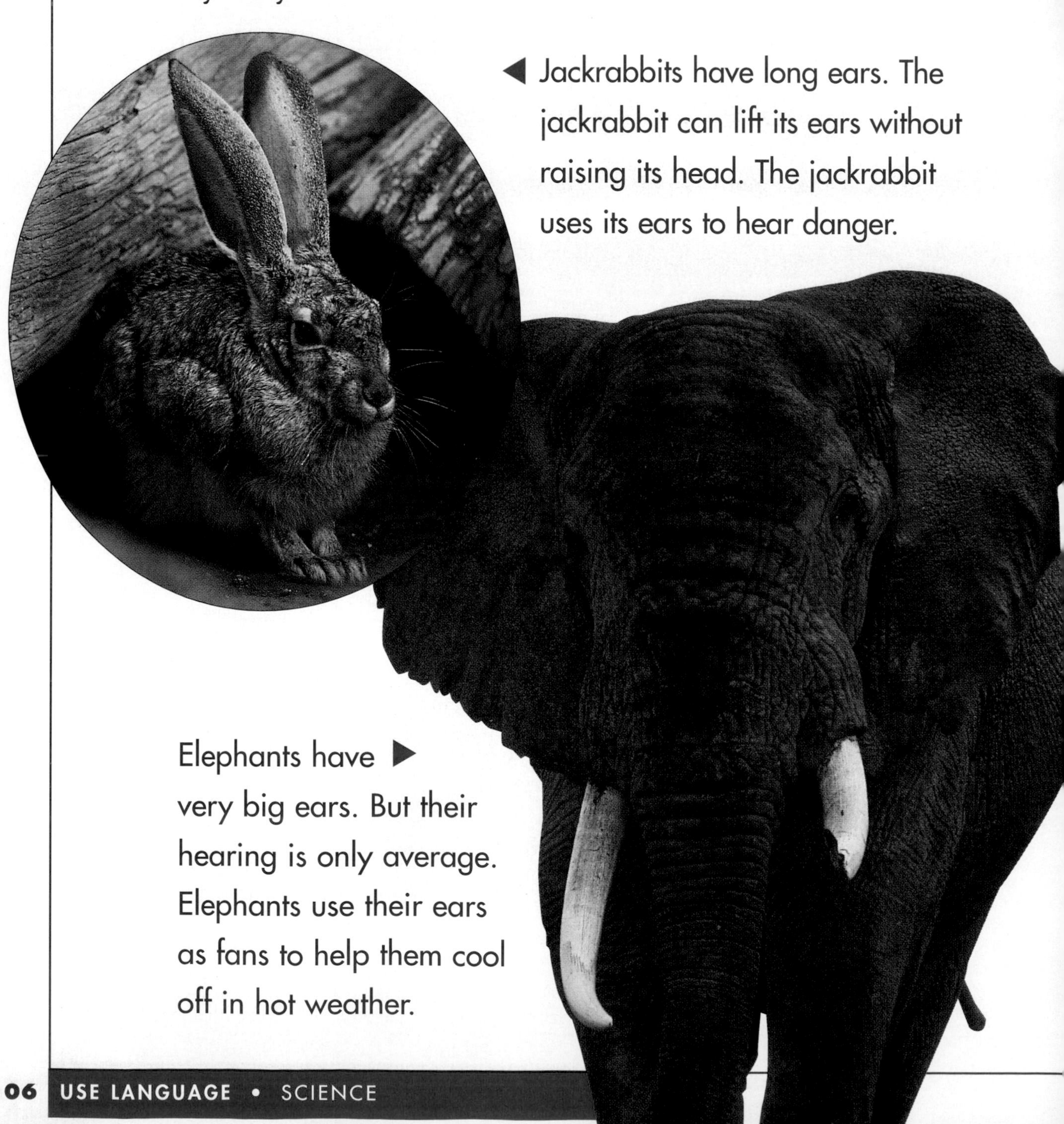

◀ Jackrabbits have long ears. The jackrabbit can lift its ears without raising its head. The jackrabbit uses its ears to hear danger.

Elephants have ▶ very big ears. But their hearing is only average. Elephants use their ears as fans to help them cool off in hot weather.

◀ German shepherds have excellent hearing. Their ears are always up and ready to hear sounds. German shepherds are good guides for blind people.

Birds have excellent hearing too. They hear through little flaps of skin that are covered with feathers. Some birds, like owls, use their hearing to find food at night. ▼

Think About It

Why do animals need good hearing?

How well do you hear?

Find out how well you hear in each of your ears.

Things You Need

- paper
- pencil
- chair
- tape measure
- ticking clock or timer

1. Make a chart.

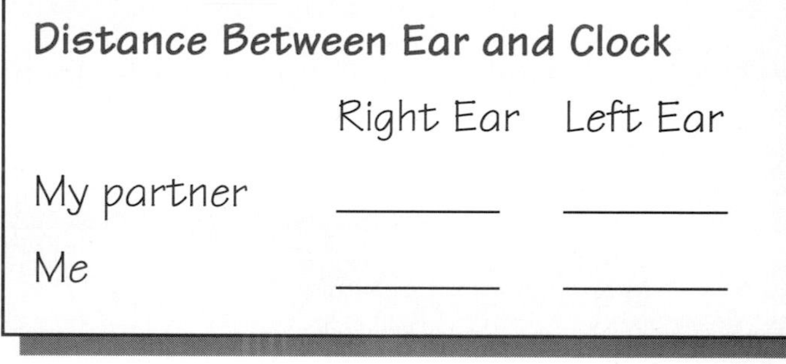

Distance Between Ear and Clock

	Right Ear	Left Ear
My partner	______	______
Me	______	______

2. Have your partner sit in a chair facing the wall. Tell your partner to cover his or her right ear.

3. Hold a ticking clock. Walk slowly away from your partner. Tell your partner to say "Stop" when he or she can't hear the clock.

4. When your partner says "Stop," put the clock on the floor where you are standing.

5. Measure the distance from the clock to your partner. Write down the distance.

6. Repeat steps 2–5 with the left ear.

7. Change places with your partner. Repeat steps 2–6.

Try It Out

Do you think you would hear better using both ears? Why? Do the experiment again to find out.

Sounds, Inventions, and Communication

Many things have been invented that help people communicate. People communicate when they share news or information.

People who do not hear well use **hearing aids.** Hearing aids make sounds easier to hear.

People use the **radio** to hear music and information.

People use **television** to see and hear programs and information.

People use the **telephone** to talk with others.

People use **microphones** to talk to large groups of people. Microphones help make sounds louder.

Write About It

Which communication inventions interest you most? Why?

What other inventions help people communicate? Make a list.

cellular phone

computer

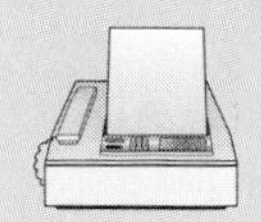

fax machine

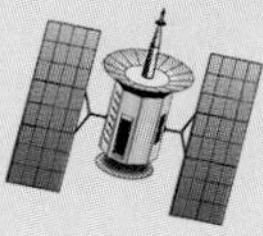

satellite

BE GOOD TO YOUR EARS!

Come listen to UPBEAT!

The music is so good that your ears will thank you!

Editorial by Ana Martínez

Noise Alert

The band *Upbeat* is coming to town. Cover your ears! The band's music is very loud. The music is so loud that it can hurt your ears. You may even lose some of your hearing. Be kind to your ears! Stay home.

Try It Out

Make a poster for your favorite musical group. It might be a rock band or a school chorus.

Do Your **Ears** Hang Low?

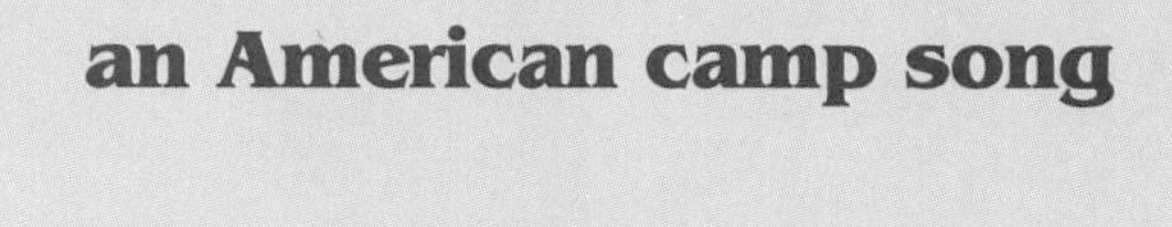

an American camp song

Do your ears hang low,

Do they wobble to and fro?

Can you tie them in a knot,

Can you tie them in a bow?

Can you fling them over your shoulder

Like a Continental soldier,

Do your ears hang low?

Tell what you learned.

1. Why is sound important to living things?

2. List the communication inventions you used yesterday.

3. You read about Upbeat. Would you want this band to come to where you live? Why or why not?

4. Name one interesting thing that you learned about sound. Why was this interesting to you?

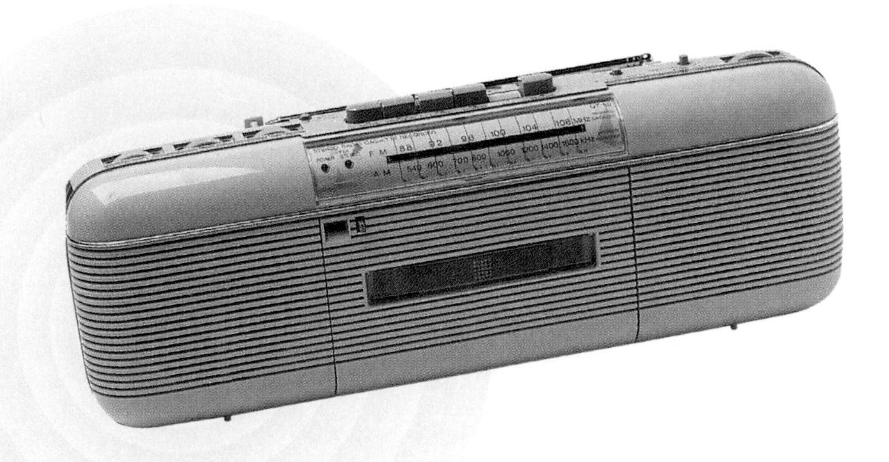

Plants, Animals, and Climate

Tell what you know.

What place do you see in each picture?

What kinds of weather does each place have?

What kinds of plants and animals can live in each place?

Word Bank

cold
dry
hot
shady
sunny

Talk About It

Think about the country your family comes from. What is the weather like there? What plants and animals live there?

Deserts and Forests

A **desert** is a place that gets very little rain. Most plants need a lot of rain to grow. A cactus does not. A cactus can grow in a desert.

Many deserts are sandy. Other deserts have dry soil and rocks.

Most deserts are very hot. Other deserts are very cold. The kind of weather a place has is its **climate.**

The climate of the desert in this picture is hot and dry.

A **forest** is a place that gets a lot of rain. Many different trees and plants grow in a forest.

Some forests are hot and rainy. Some forests are warm and sunny. Other forests are cool and shady.

Some forests stay the same all year. In other forests, trees lose their leaves in winter.

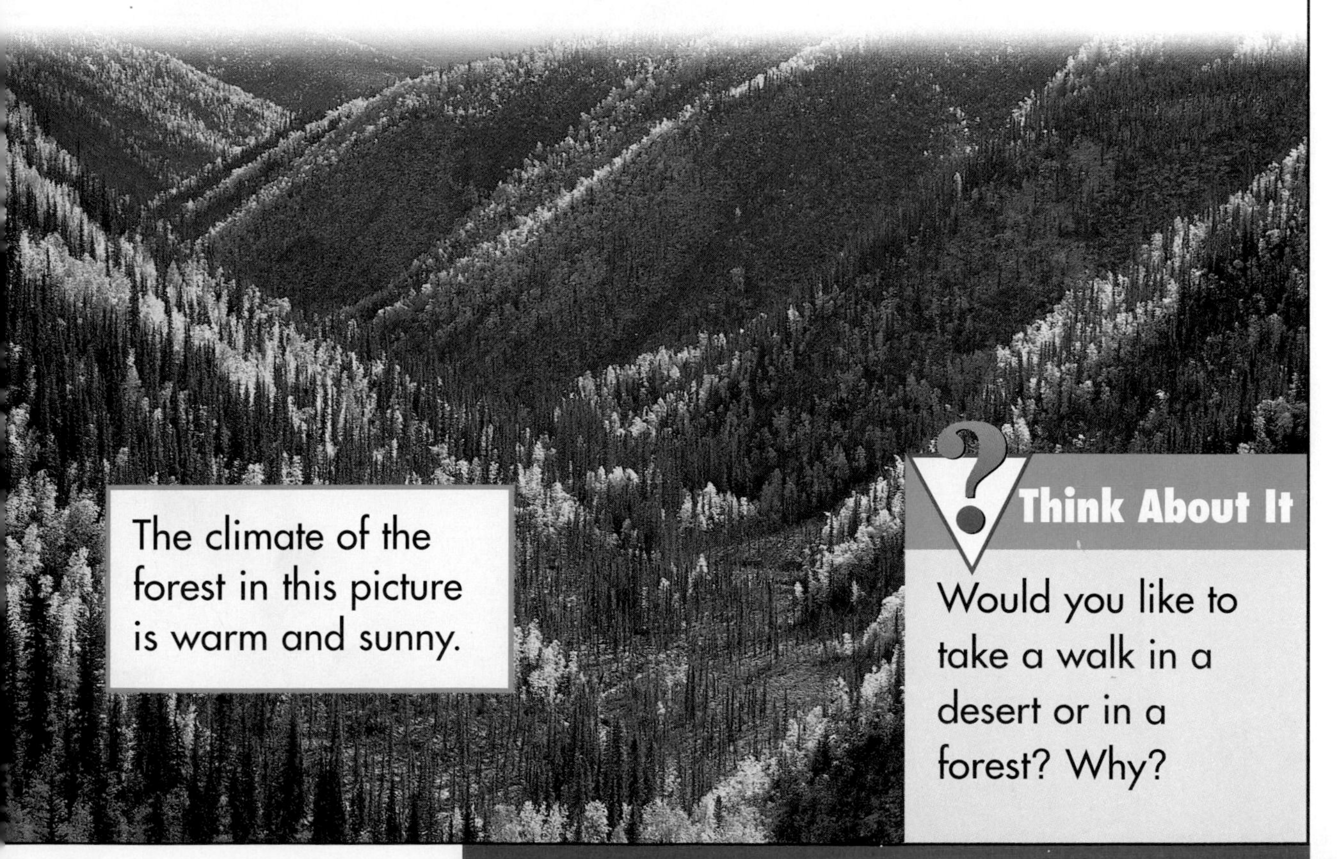

The climate of the forest in this picture is warm and sunny.

Think About It

Would you like to take a walk in a desert or in a forest? Why?

How can a cactus live in a desert?

A cactus has special parts that help it live in a desert.

This is a saguaro cactus.

1 A cactus has roots that spread out from its stem. The roots are near the top of the ground. When it rains, the roots take in the water quickly.

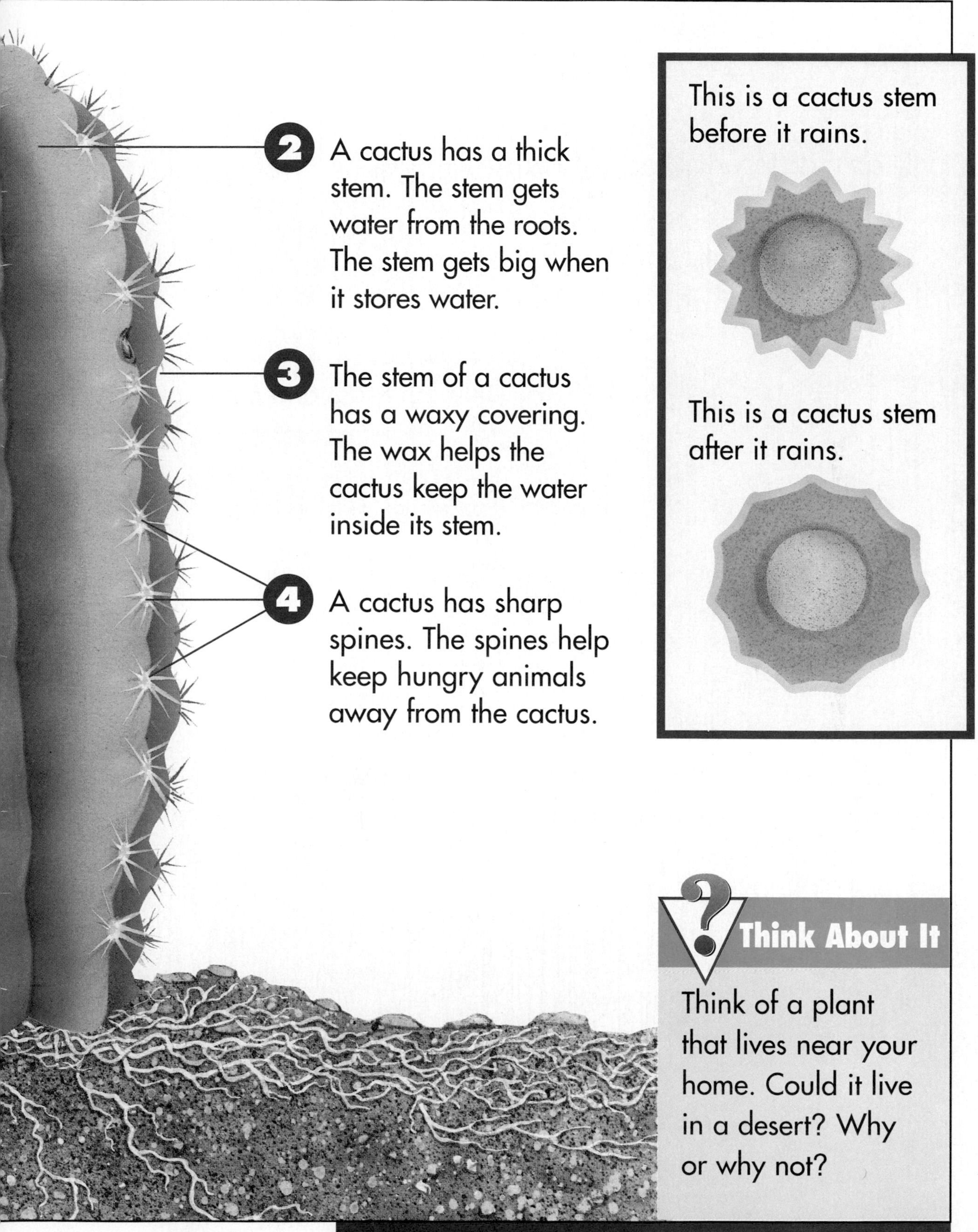

2 A cactus has a thick stem. The stem gets water from the roots. The stem gets big when it stores water.

3 The stem of a cactus has a waxy covering. The wax helps the cactus keep the water inside its stem.

4 A cactus has sharp spines. The spines help keep hungry animals away from the cactus.

This is a cactus stem before it rains.

This is a cactus stem after it rains.

Think About It

Think of a plant that lives near your home. Could it live in a desert? Why or why not?

How do animals live in a forest?

Many different kinds of animals live in the forest. It is easy for them to find food, water, and a place to live in spring, summer, and fall.

Some forests are cold and snowy in winter. Then it is not easy for animals to find food, water, and a place to live.

Deer dig under the snow to find grass to eat. They eat snow to get water.

Rabbits dig holes in the snow to keep warm.

Chipmunks stay in a nest under the ground. They eat acorns they found in the summer.

Write About It

Draw a picture of animals in a forest in the summer or winter. Write a title for your drawing. Then tell a partner about it.

Taking Care of Animals

Animals that are sick or hurt need lots of care. People can take their pets to an animal hospital to get help.

Dr. Marino is a **veterinarian.** People bring their pets to him. He checks the animals to see if they are in good health. He helps animals that are sick and hurt feel better.

Joan is a **volunteer** at an animal hospital. A volunteer works without pay. Joan cleans the cages. She feeds and pets the animals. She helps Dr. Marino.

Word Bank

cat
dog
fish
hamster
parakeet
rabbit

Think About It

Name a pet you have or would like to have. How would you take care of it? What would you do if your pet got sick?

Desert Animals

by Elsa Posell

Reader's Tip
A title often tells you what a reading is about. What is this selection about?

Many desert animals are different from animals found in other places. Desert animals can live in a hot, dry place.

Some desert animals sleep under rocks all day. Others burrow under the ground all day. They keep out of the hot sun.

Language Tip: Vocabulary
Burrow means "to dig a hole in the ground."

camel

Some deserts have sandstorms. Most desert animals can close their nostrils. This helps keep sand out of their noses. They can keep the sand out of their eyes and ears, too.

Language Tip: Use Clues from Other Sentences
What are *nostrils*? Use the next sentence to figure out the meaning of this word.

Desert animals have tough skin over their lips. They have strong teeth. They can eat the spiny, prickly plants of the desert.

Strategy Tip: Use Pictures for Meaning
Look at the picture to understand what a *spiny, prickly plant* looks like.

barrel cactus

Strategy Tip:
Use Pictures for Meaning
Look at the picture to understand the meaning of *scaly*.

collared lizard

Many different lizards live in the desert. Their skins are scaly.

desert skink

Many of them are the color of the ground or of plants. This helps protect them from their enemies. Enemies cannot see them easily. Lizards also run very fast.

Language Tip: Vocabulary
Enemies are not friends. A lizard's enemies will try to hurt or kill it.

horned toad

The horned toad is not a toad. It is really a lizard. Its head is covered with spines like horns. These are hard and rough. Few animals try to eat this lizard.

Strategy Tip: Stop and Think
Why do few animals try to eat the horned toad?

The horned toad is spotted brown and gray. It is hard to see.

Strategy Tip: Stop and Think
What do you learn about a *kangaroo* by reading about a kangaroo rat?

The kangaroo rat is also found in the desert. Its hind legs and tail are very long. Its front legs are short. It uses its front paws as hands and hops like a kangaroo. It carries food in a pocket in each side of its mouth.

kangaroo rat

desert turtle

The desert turtle has two water sacs in its body. It stores water in them. It drinks only about once or twice a year. Instead of teeth, its jaws are like small saws. It cuts food with them.

Language Tip: Vocabulary
A *saw* is a tool used to cut trees and wood.

sidewinder rattlesnake

Many snakes live in the desert. Some are harmless. Some are dangerous. The sidewinders and diamondbacks are rattlesnakes. They are poisonous.

Language Tip: Antonyms
Harmless and *dangerous* have opposite meanings. *Harmless* means "not going to hurt you." What does *dangerous* mean?

The roadrunner is a bird of the desert. It is about two feet long from beak to tail. Its legs are long and strong. It is a fast runner. It can keep up with a car going twenty miles an hour.

roadrunner

Vocabulary Tip: Stop and Think
How do you think the *roadrunner* got its name?

THE DESERT

by Eucario Mendez
written when he was in 6th grade

As I walk in the desert
I see a coral snake passing by,
and the bright sun shines the day.
I hear birds singing on a
mesquite tree. I hear animals
crying for food and water.
I feel a strong breeze passing by,
and the animals come to me
so I can touch them.
So, next time you are in
a desert, like me, see things,
feel things, and hear things.

Tell what you learned.

1. Make a chart. List some things that are true about a desert. List some things that are true about a forest.

	Plants	Animals	Weather
Desert			
Forest			

2. Why can a cactus live in a desert?

3. Name an animal that lives in the desert. Tell what you learned about that animal.

4. Think about a place outdoors where you walk. What do you see there? What do you hear? What do you feel? Make a list.

Weather and People

Tell what you know.

What kind of weather do you see in each picture?

Word Bank

cool
foggy
rainy
snowy
stormy
warm
windy

Talk About It

What has the weather been like this week where you live?

Weather affects the way people live.

People can do different things in different kinds of weather.

When the weather is warm, people can grow fruits and vegetables.

On warm, sunny days, people like to do things outside. They can go swimming, ride bikes, and have picnics.

When it rains, most people do not do things outside.

◀ When the weather is cold, people try to keep warm. They can sled, ice skate, and ski. If there is a big snowstorm, people may not be able to leave their homes.

◀ When the weather is very hot, people try to stay cool. In some countries, people close their shops during the hottest part of the day.

Think About It

What kind of weather do you like? Why?

What things do you like to do in different kinds of weather?

Dressing for the Weather

People wear different clothes in different kinds of weather.

◀ People wear lots of clothes when it is cold outside.

◀ People do not wear as many clothes when it is hot outside.

◀ In hot, sunny places, people often wear hats to protect them from the sun.

◀ In desert lands, some people wear long robes and cover their heads to protect them from the sun and blowing sand.

◀ Many people wear raincoats and carry umbrellas on rainy days.

Think About It

Think about the weather in the country your family is from. Think about the weather where you live now. What is different about the way you dress?

Climates Around the World

Look at the map of the world. Look at the **map key.** Each color shows a different climate.

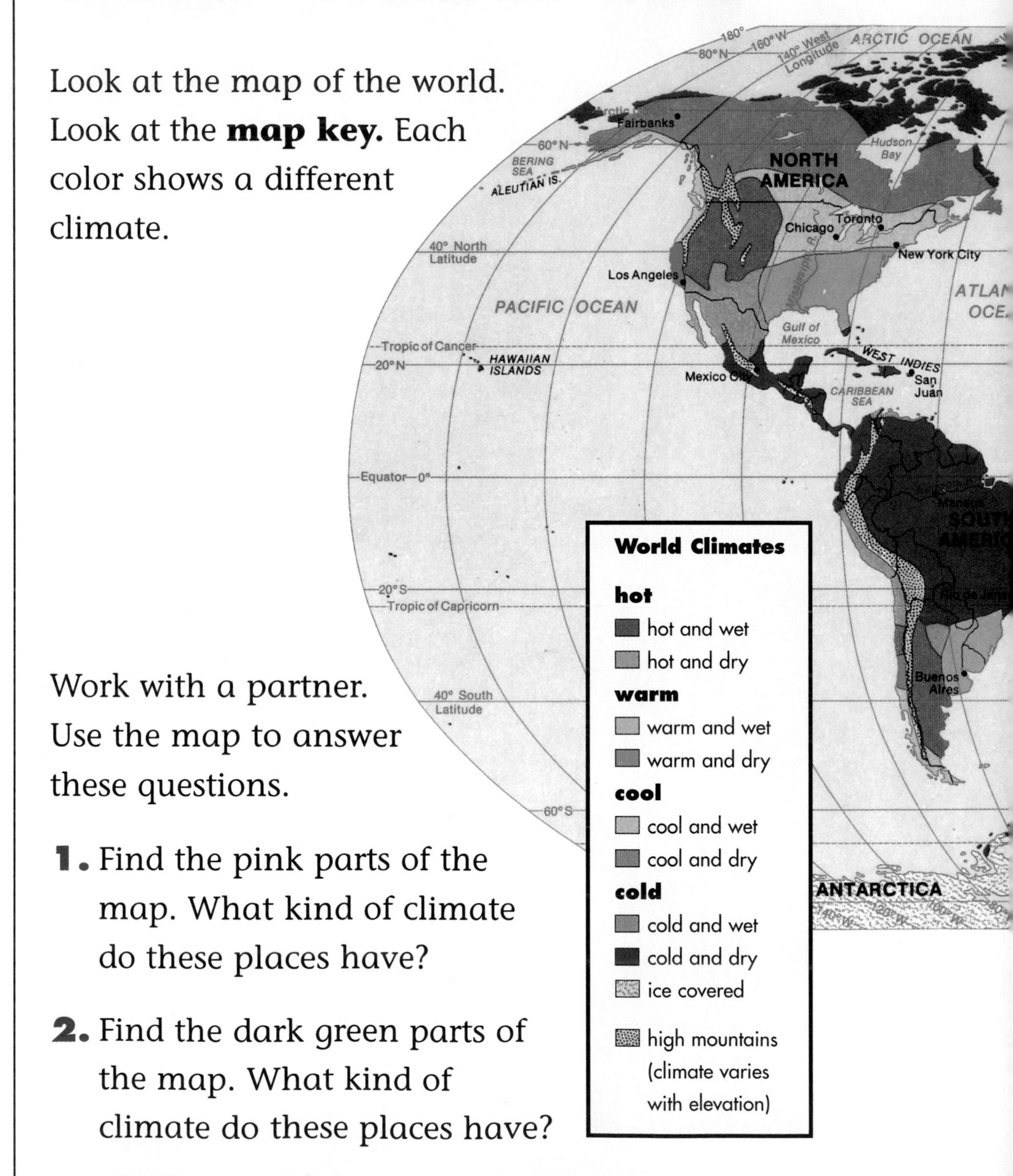

Work with a partner. Use the map to answer these questions.

1. Find the pink parts of the map. What kind of climate do these places have?

2. Find the dark green parts of the map. What kind of climate do these places have?

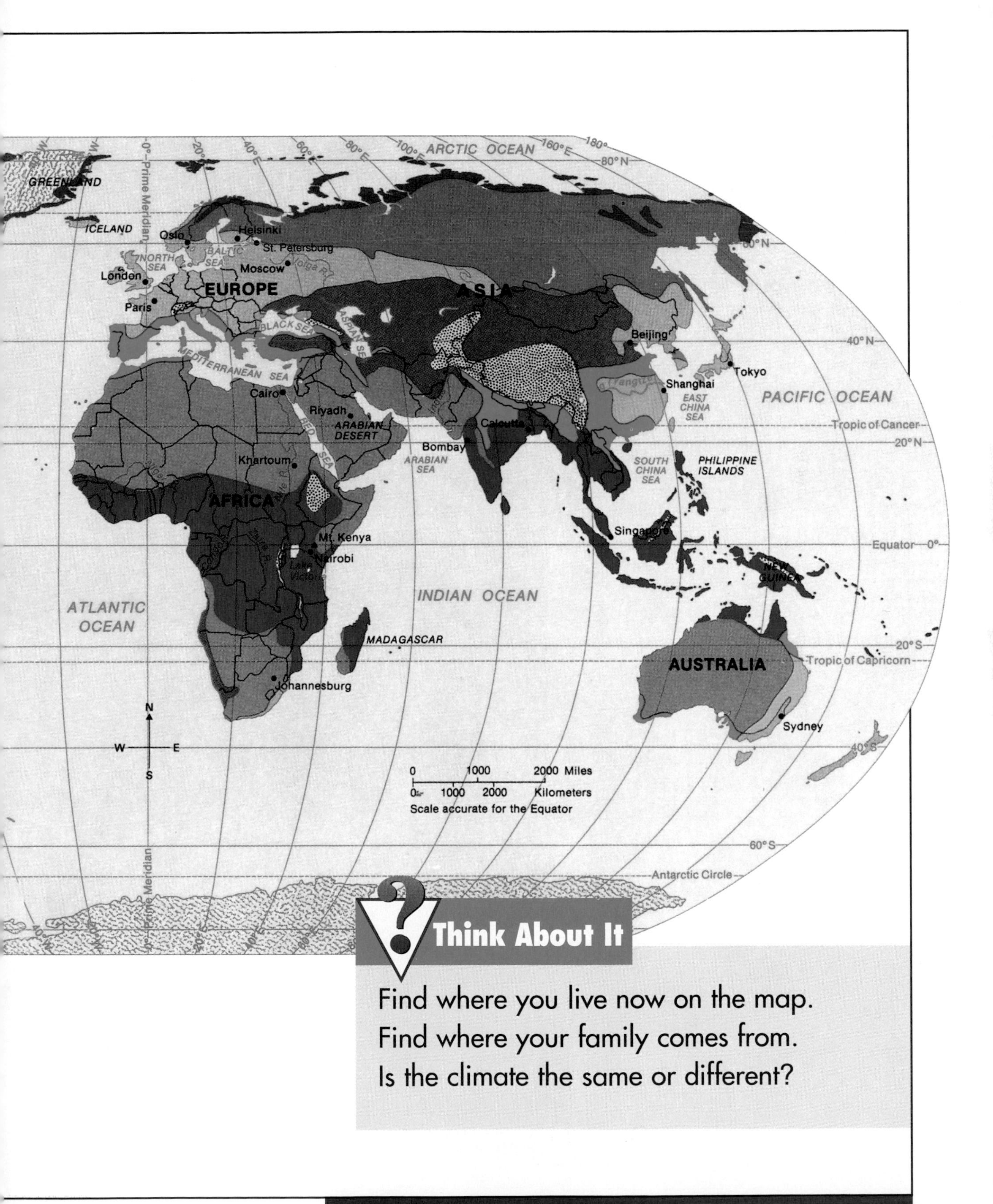

Think About It

Find where you live now on the map.
Find where your family comes from.
Is the climate the same or different?

Safety First

Here are some things you should do to stay healthy in hot weather.

1. Wear loose, light clothes.

2. Drink plenty of water.

3. Wear a hat in the sun.

4. Put on sunscreen or lotion.

5. Rest if you feel very hot.

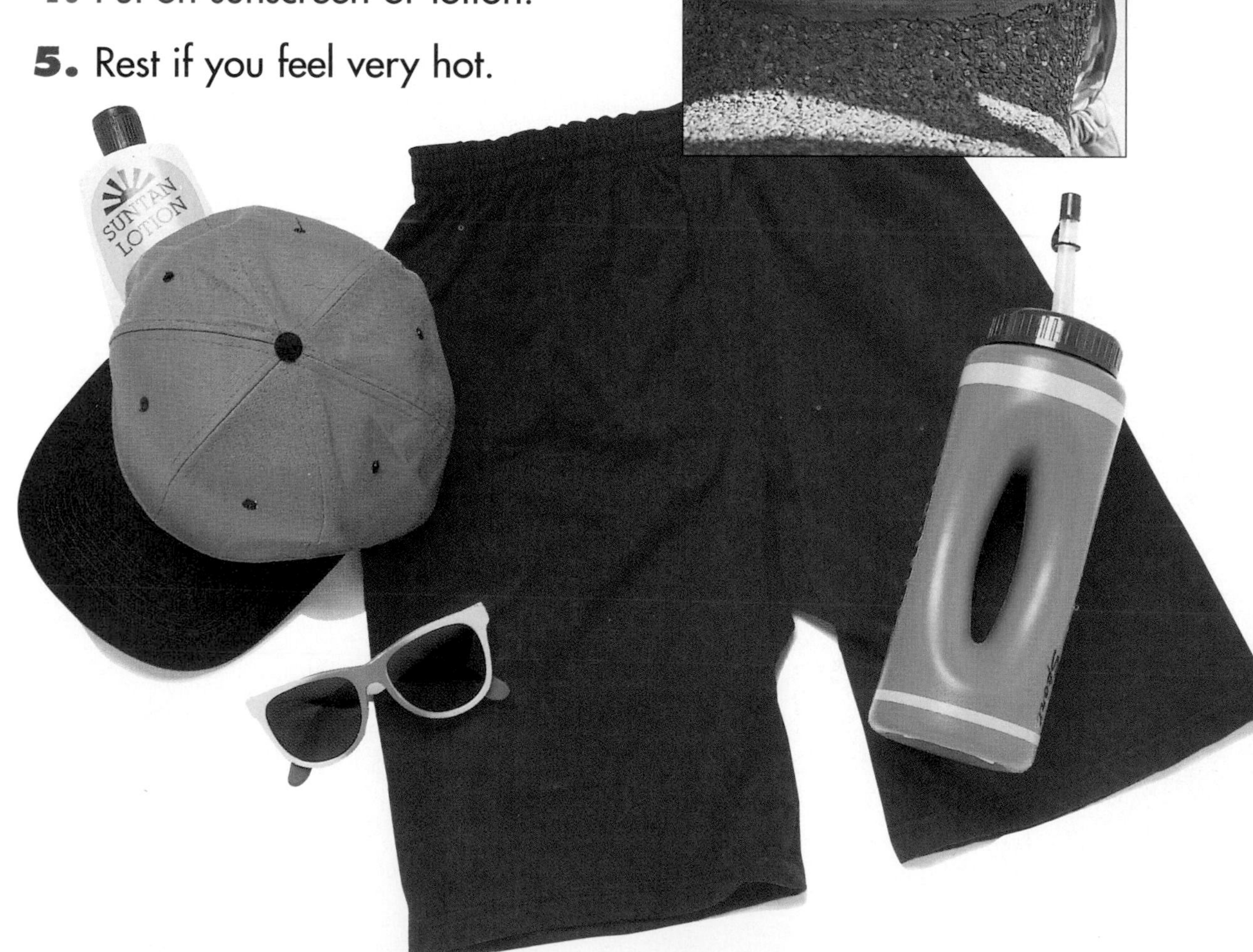

Here are some things you should do to stay healthy in cold weather.

1. Wear warm clothes when you go outside.
2. Wear shoes or boots that keep your feet dry and warm.
3. Wear a hat. You lose body heat through the top of your head.
4. Don't stay outside for a long time if it is very cold.

Write About It

Write two or three rules to follow in rainy weather.

My Mother's Got Me Bundled Up

by Jack Prelutsky

My mother's got me bundled up
in tons of winter clothes,
you could not recognize me
if I did not have a nose.
I'd wear much less, but she'd get mad
if I dared disobey her,
so I stay wrapped from head to toe
in layer after layer.

I am wearing extra sweaters,

I am wearing extra socks,

my galoshes are so heavy

that my ankles seem like rocks.

I am wearing scarves and earmuffs,

I am wearing itchy pants,

my legs feel like they're swarming

with a million tiny ants.

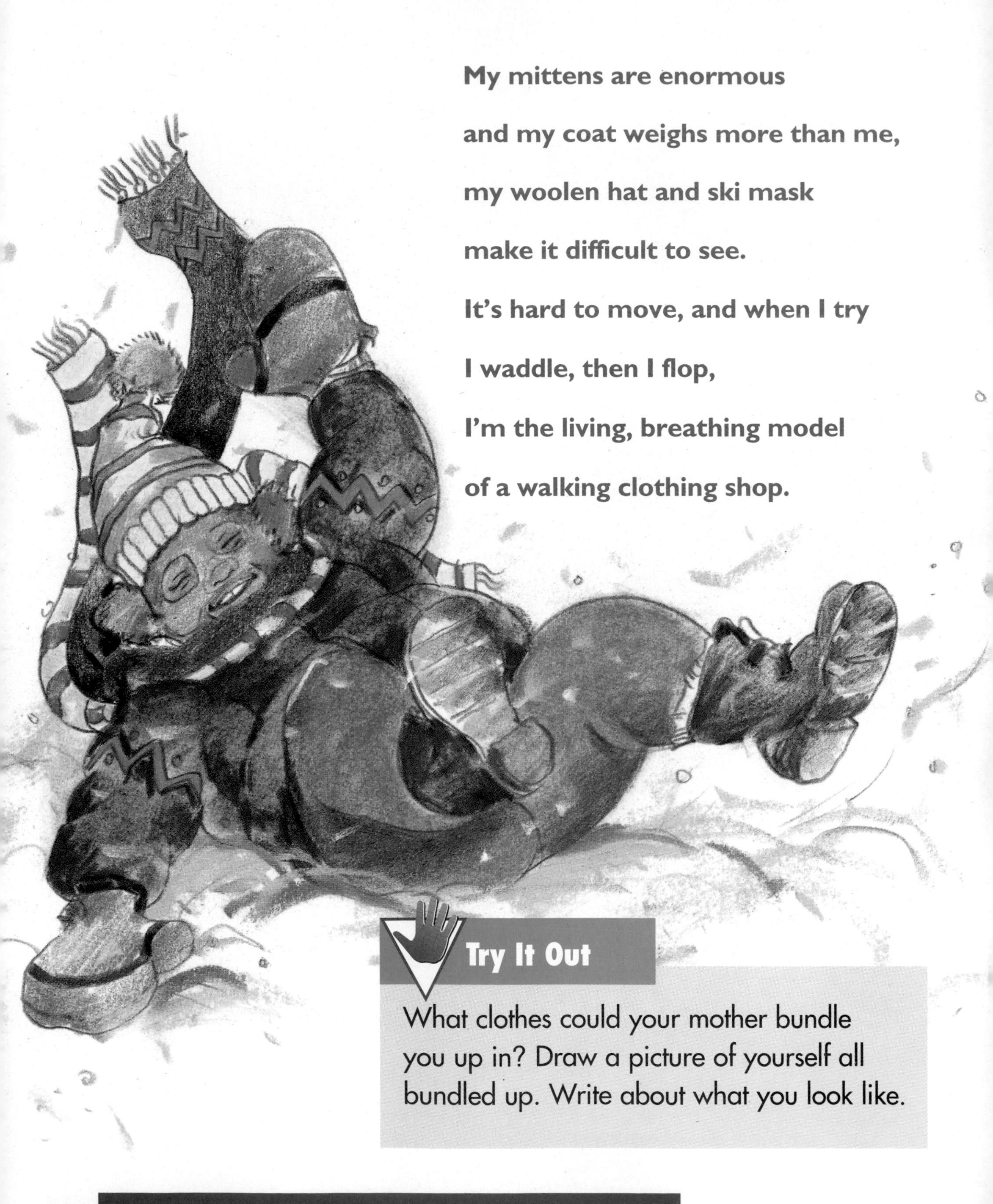

My mittens are enormous

and my coat weighs more than me,

my woolen hat and ski mask

make it difficult to see.

It's hard to move, and when I try

I waddle, then I flop,

I'm the living, breathing model

of a walking clothing shop.

Try It Out

What clothes could your mother bundle you up in? Draw a picture of yourself all bundled up. Write about what you look like.

Tell what you learned.

1. How do people dress differently in hot weather and in cold weather?

2. Draw a picture and write about what you might do on a rainy day. Then draw a picture and write about what you might do on a warm, sunny day.

3. Name some of the kinds of clothes the child has to wear in "My Mother's Got Me Bundled Up." Why doesn't the child like to wear them?

4. What did you enjoy most about this chapter? Why?

CHAPTER 9

What Shelters Are Made Of

Tell what you know.

People's homes are their shelters. What kinds of homes do you see in the pictures?

Word Bank

- apartment building
- mobile home
- house
- houseboat

Talk About It

Why do you need shelter?

What kind of home do you live in?

Materials for Homes

Homes are made of different **materials.**

Some homes are made of mud.

Some homes are made of wood.

Some homes are made of snow.

Some homes are made of stone.

Parts of homes are made of different materials.

This porch is made of wood.

These windows are made of glass.

These steps are made of cement.

Think About It

How are the homes in the pictures like your home? How are they different?

What materials is your home made of?

Finding Materials Long Ago

Long ago, people used materials they could easily find to build their homes. People who lived in different places built their homes with different materials.

If grass and dirt were easy to ▶ find, people built their homes with **sod.** Sod is packed grass and dirt. This house is made of sod.

If stone and mud were easy to find, people built their homes of stone and mud. This house is made of stone and mud. ▼

If trees were easy to find, people built their homes with wood. This house is made of **logs.** A log is a tree that someone has cut down. People filled the spaces between the logs with mud and moss. ▼

If sand and clay were easy to find, people built their homes with **adobe.** Adobe is a mixture of sandy clay, water, and straw. This house is made of adobe. ▼

Think About It

Why didn't all people use the same materials to build their homes?

How did homes change over time?

As people learned more about how to build, their homes changed. Look at the time line to see how people's homes changed through the years.

500,000 years ago

Some people lived in caves.

2,500 years ago

Some people built their homes in the sides of cliffs.

500 years ago

Some people in Europe used stone to build castles.

Today

Some people use steel to build apartment buildings.

Think About It

Think about the homes in your community. Do some look older than others?

How have the homes in your community changed over time?

A Beaver's Lodge

Like people, animals build shelters from the materials they find around them. A beaver uses trees and mud to build its shelter. A beaver's shelter is called a **lodge.**

1. First, the beaver cuts down trees and branches with its strong front teeth.

2. Next, the beaver piles up the branches.

4 Finally, the beaver puts mud and leaves between the branches and logs. The mud and leaves keep the beaver's lodge warm when the weather gets cold.

3 Then, the beaver uses its teeth to make tunnels. The tunnels help the beaver get in and out of its lodge.

Write About It

Think about another animal that builds a shelter.

Draw a picture of the shelter.

List the materials the animal uses to build the shelter.

Houses and Homes

by Ann Morris

photographs by Ken Heyman

Strategy Tip: Think Before You Read
The world is full of many different kinds of houses. What kinds of houses do you know about?

The world is full of houses . . .

big houses

little houses

bright houses

white houses

houses that move

and houses that stay in a row

Language Tip: Vocabulary

In a row means "one next to the other."

or all alone

filled with families

just right for one.

Strategy Tip: Stop and Think

What kinds of houses have you read about so far? What can you do if you don't remember?

Language Tip: Vocabulary
Handy means "near you." People use materials that are close to where they live.

Build your house with what is handy...

wood or stone

or straw or mud

or almost anything at all.

Strategy Tip:
Use What You Know
What other things have you seen that people weave?

Weave it

nail it

tie it with rope.

Build it on stilts!

Reader's Tip
People who live near water often build their houses high above the water.

Let in the air to keep it cool.

Fill in the cracks to keep it warm.

Fill it with love

and make it a home.

Language Tip: Idioms

Fill it with love means "have a lot of love in the house."

HOUSES

by Aileen Fisher

Houses are faces
(haven't you found?)
with their hats in the air,
and their necks in the ground.

Windows are noses,
windows are eyes,
and doors are the mouths
of a suitable size.

And a porch — or the place
where porches begin —
is just like a mustache
shading the chin.

Tell what you learned.

1. Make a chart like this one. Write the names of different kinds of homes and the materials they are made of.

Homes	Materials

2. Think about a favorite house from *Houses and Homes*. Draw a picture of the house. Write about why you like it. Share your work with a friend.

3. Talk to an older family member about the home he or she lived in when he or she was your age. How is your home different? How is it the same?

4. What was the most interesting thing you learned about in this chapter? What would you like to know more about?

How Shelters Are Built

Tell what you know.

These are building tools and materials.

Which of these tools and materials have you seen someone use?

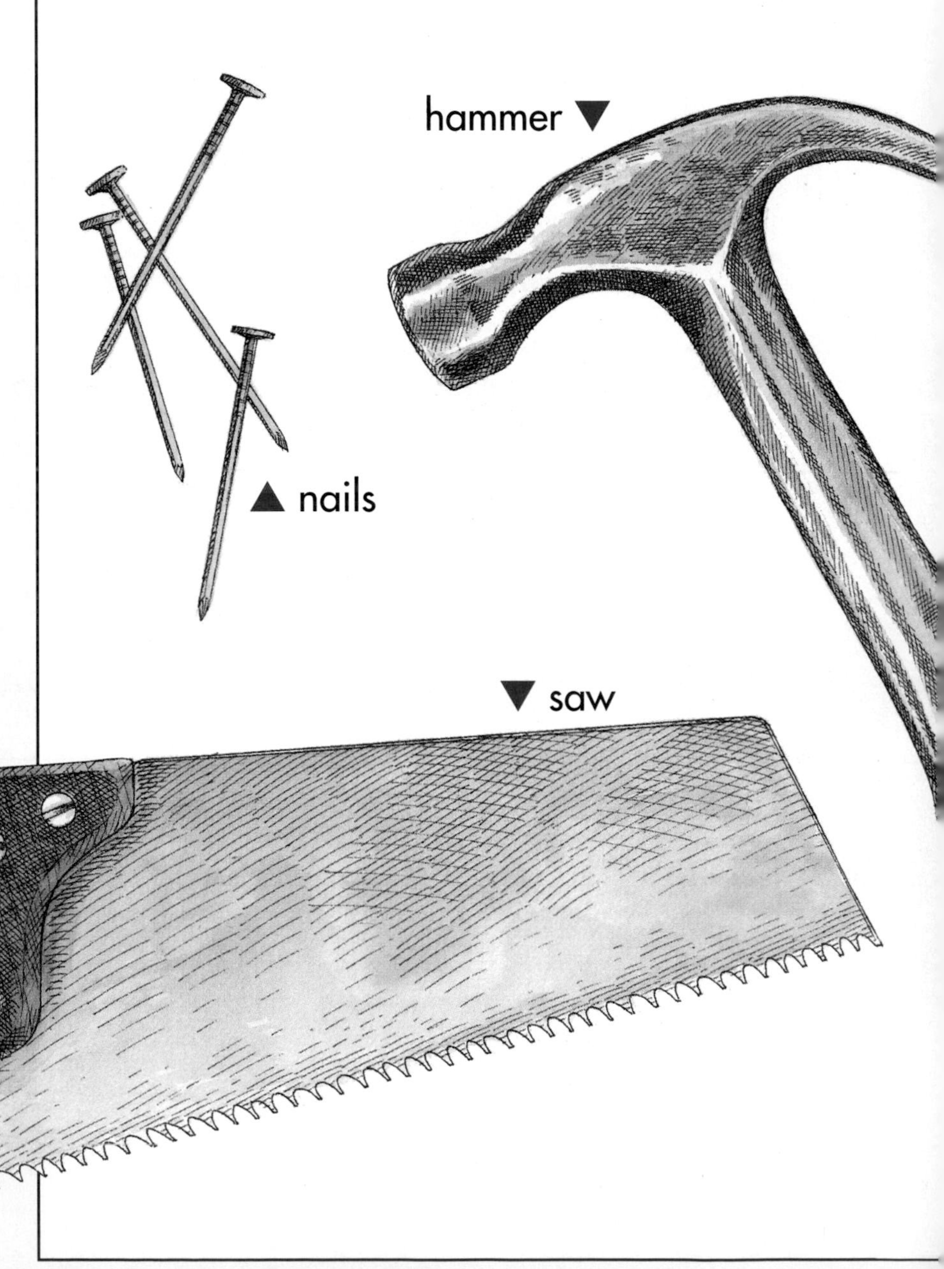

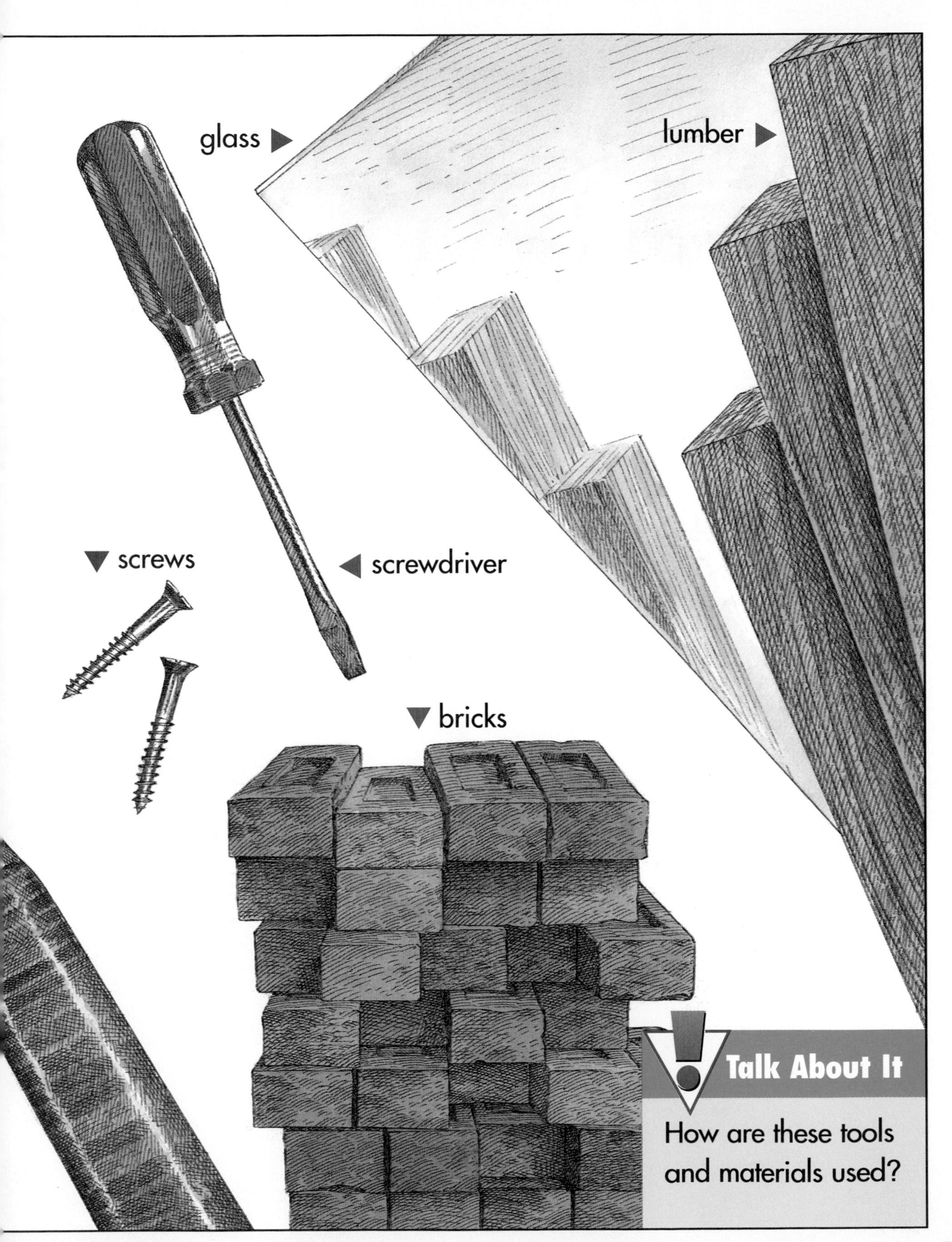

Talk About It

How are these tools and materials used?

Where do building materials come from?

People use materials that come from **natural resources** to build. A natural resource is something that comes from the earth and can be used by living things.

People use **lumber** to build houses. Lumber comes from trees.

People use **nails** to hold the lumber together. Nails are made of steel. Steel comes from iron found in iron mines.

People use **bricks** to build houses. Clay and rock mixed together make bricks.

People use **mortar** to hold the bricks together. Cement, sand, and water mixed together make mortar.

Think About It

What building materials do you see in your school?

What materials do you see in the place where you live?

How are bricks made?

Bricks are made from clay and rock.

Here are the steps for making bricks.

Clay and rock are ground into very small pieces.

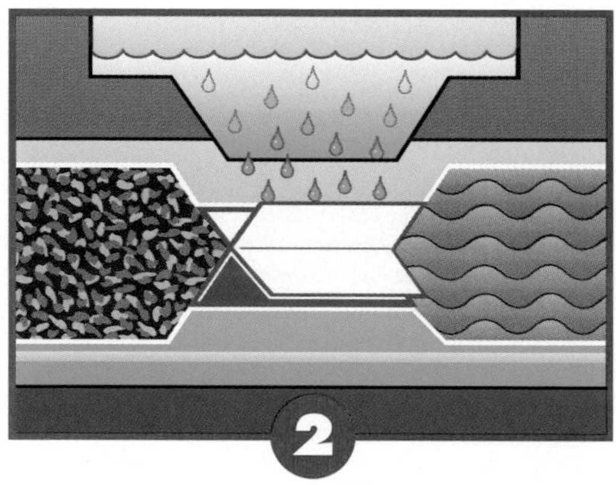

The ground-up clay and rock is mixed with water. The mixture becomes a stiff paste.

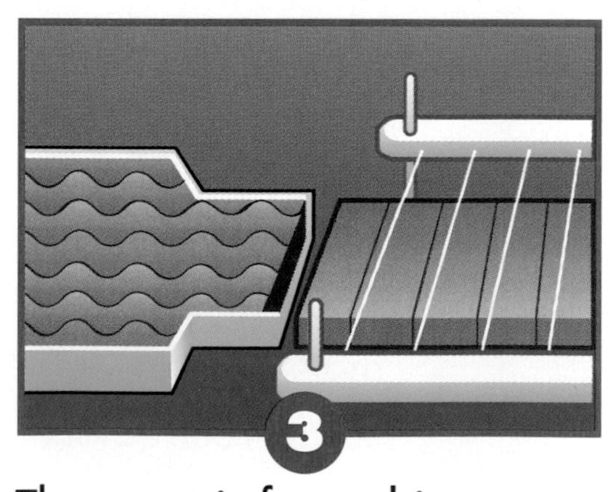

The paste is formed into blocks. Then the blocks are cut into bricks.

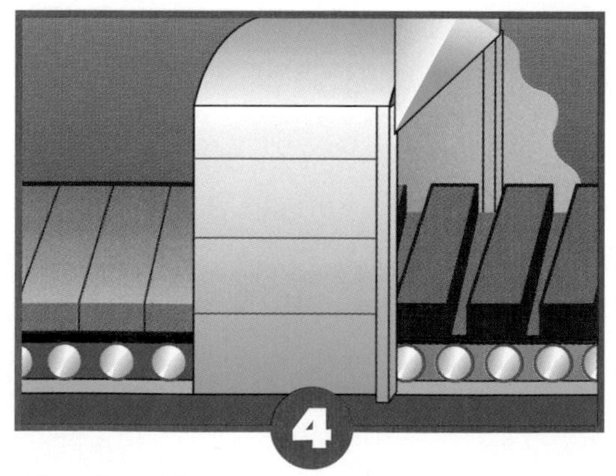

The bricks are baked in very hot ovens.

How is glass made?

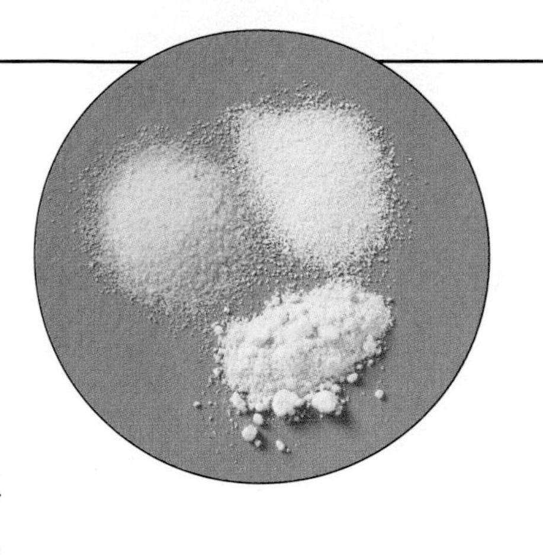

Glass is made up of **sand**, **lime**, and **soda**. Sand is a natural resource. Lime and soda come from natural resources. Lime comes from limestone. Soda comes from salt.

Here are the steps for making glass.

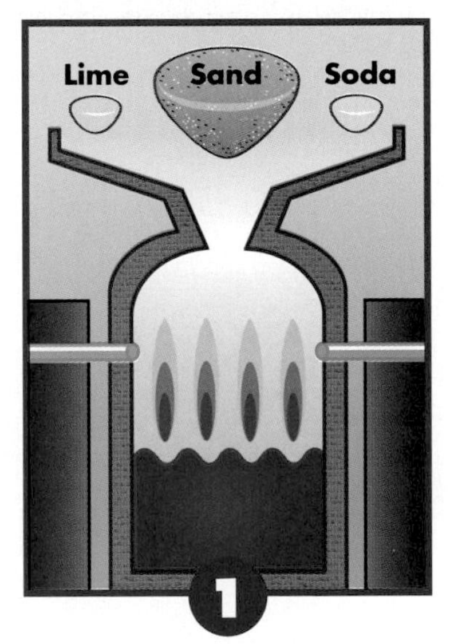

A large amount of sand is mixed and heated with small amounts of lime and soda.

After the mixture cools, it is shaped into glass.

Word Bank

bottle

dishes

eyeglasses

vase

window

What's made of glass? How many different kinds of things can you think of?

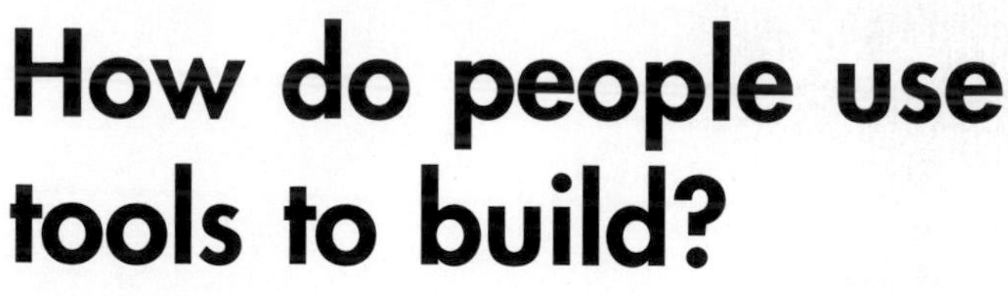

How do people use tools to build?

The builders in this picture are using **simple machines** to build a house. Simple machines have few or no moving parts.

The builders use their **energy** to make the simple machines do the work.

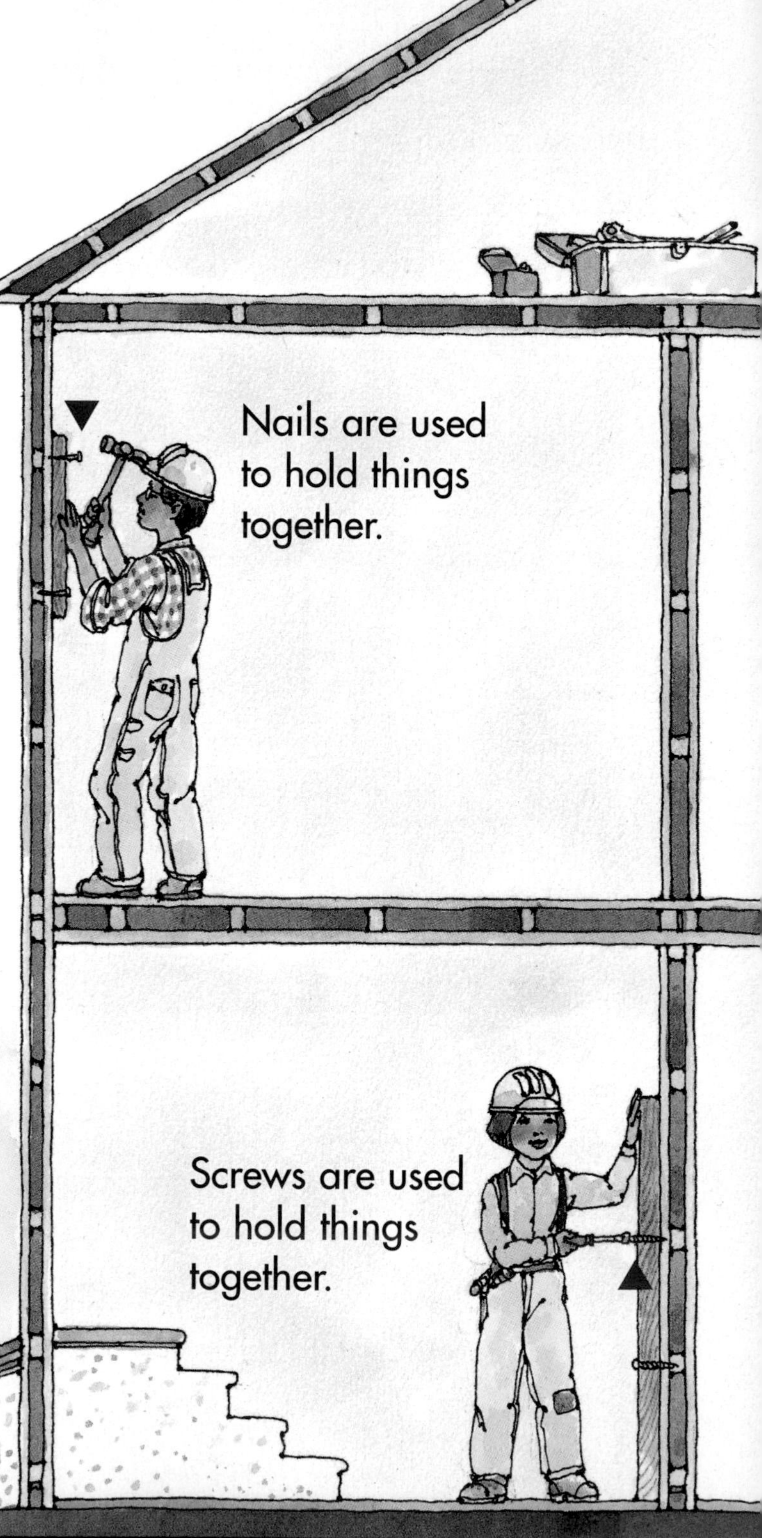

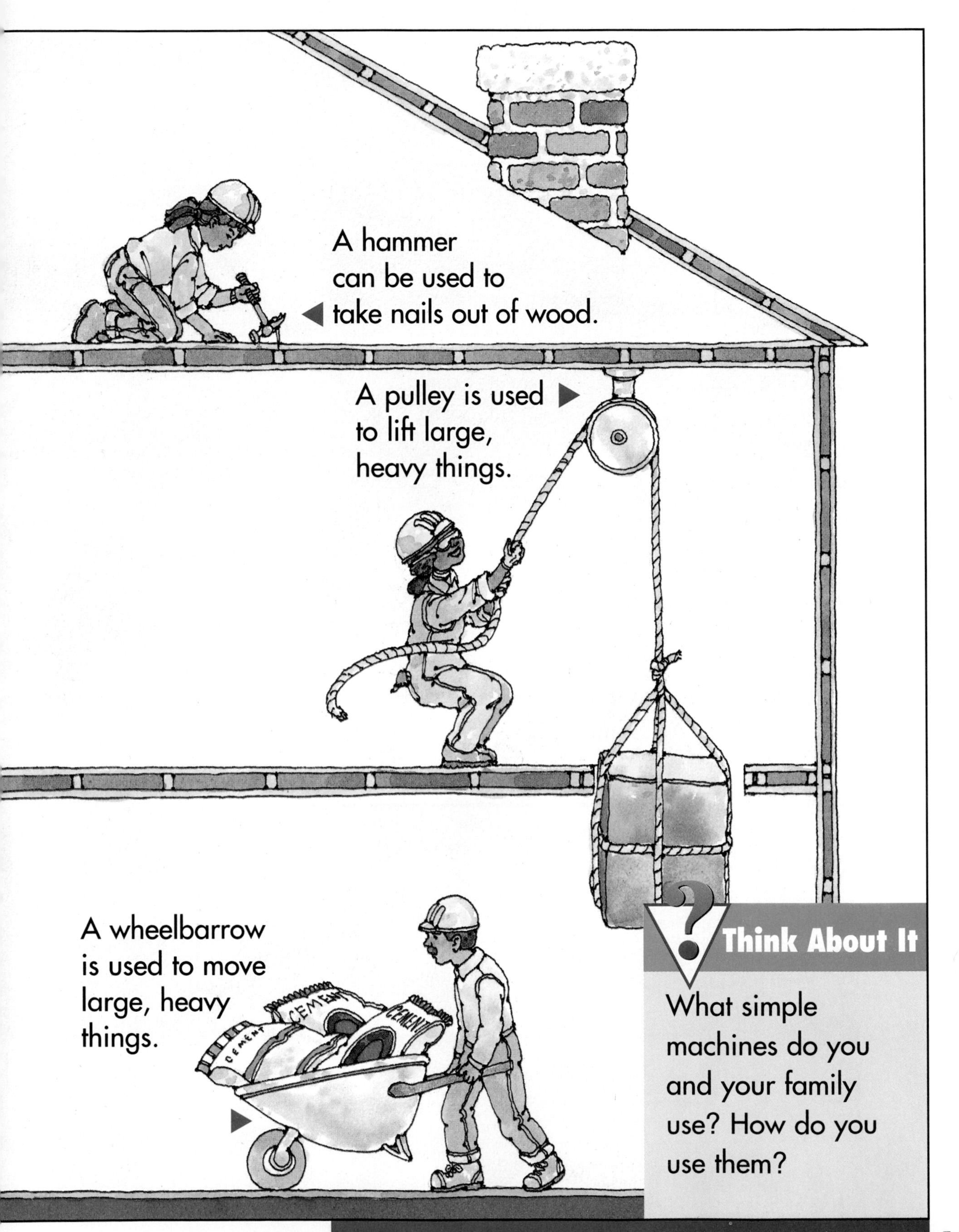

Think About It

What simple machines do you and your family use? How do you use them?

Shapes in Houses

Different parts of houses can be different shapes.

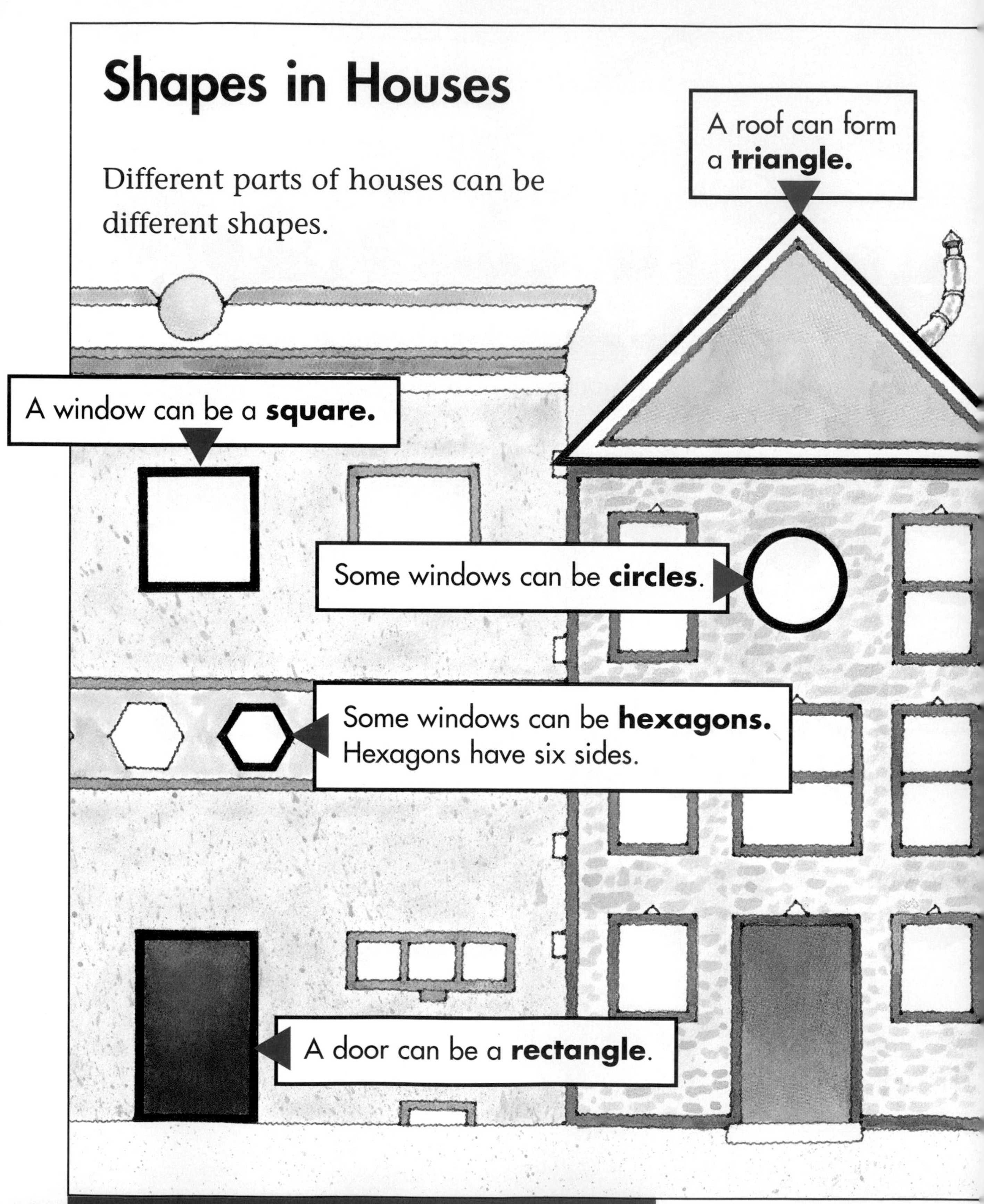

Look at these houses. How many different shapes do you see?

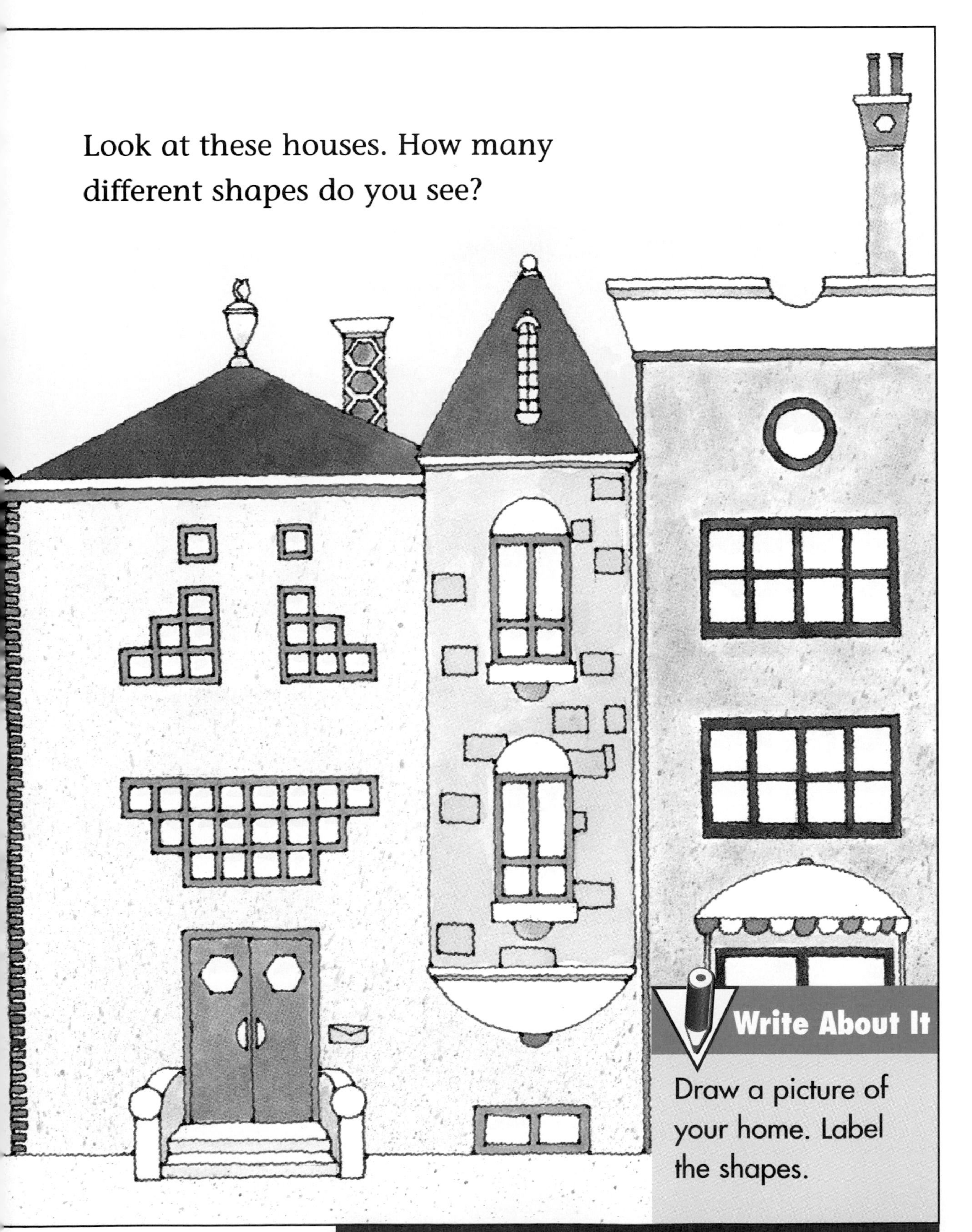

Write About It

Draw a picture of your home. Label the shapes.

My Grandma's House

by Isela Guerrero, age 10

The best thing I like in Mexico is my grandma's two-story house. On the second story there is a balcony.

In the summer, my grandma buys a big swimming pool, and we put it on the balcony. Next, we fill it with water and go swimming. At night, we take the swimming pool inside the house.

In the summer, we sleep on the balcony. In the morning, we eat breakfast and then go buy candies.

Write About It

This writer likes her grandmother's balcony. What is your favorite part of your home? Draw a picture of it. What do you like to do there?

LET'S BUILD A HOUSE

by
Lucille Wood

Let's build a house,
Let's build a house,
Let's build a house,
and **work, work, work.**

I'll be the carpenter,
I'll be the carpenter,
I'll be the carpenter,
and **saw, saw, saw.**

I'll be the roofer,
I'll be the roofer,
I'll be the roofer,
and **pound, pound, pound.**

Try It Out

Use what you know about building a house to add more lines to the song.

Tell what you learned.

1. You are going to build a house. Make a chart. List the tools and materials you will need to build the house.

Tools I Will Need	Materials I Will Need

2. Look around your school. What simple machines do you see?

3. Isela likes to go to her grandmother's house in the summer. Tell about a house you like. Why do you like it?

4. What new thing did you learn about how homes are built?

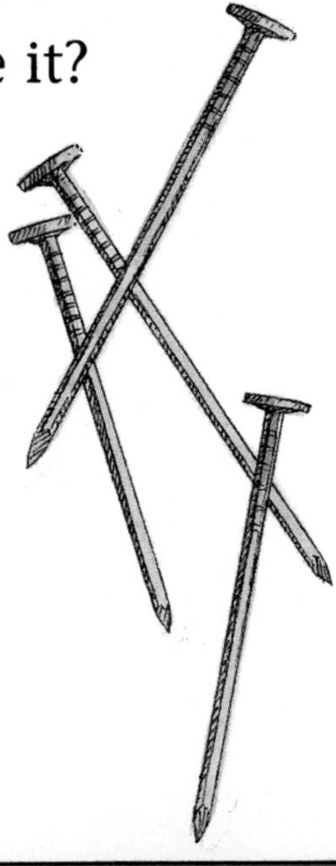

Changing the Earth

Tell what you know.

What do you see in the picture?

Word Bank

- animals
- forest
- houses
- road
- trees

Talk About It

What are the people in the picture doing?
Why are they doing this?

What will happen to the plants and animals that live in this forest?

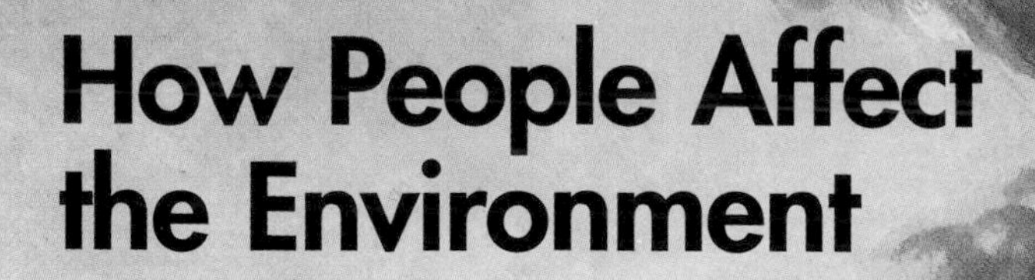

How People Affect the Environment

An **environment** is all the things that surround a living thing. Trees, water, and land are part of the environment.

When people change the environment, they usually change the homes of plants and animals. If they cut down a tree, the squirrels and birds who lived in that tree lose their homes.

Even though an animal's home may change, it can still survive. An animal needs food, water, and shelter. It also needs air and space. An animal can move to a new environment and get what it needs.

Think About It

Pretend you are an animal. Your environment is going to change soon. How do you feel about the change? What will you do?

Learning About Your Habitat

A **habitat** is a place where a plant or animal lives. Work with a team to find out about the plants and animals that live in a habitat near your school.

Things You Need

 several small plastic bags

 masking tape

string that is 1 meter long

 twigs or stones

Follow these steps.

1. Tape a piece of masking tape on each bag to use as a label.
2. Go outside with your team. Have one person hold the end of the string. Have another person hold the other end of the string and move in a circle around the first person. This circle is your habitat.
3. Use twigs or stones to mark your habitat.

4. Look at all the plants and animals inside your habitat.

5. Collect things like feathers and leaves from your habitat. Put them into the plastic bags.

6. Write what you found, where you found it, and the date you found it on the label of each bag.

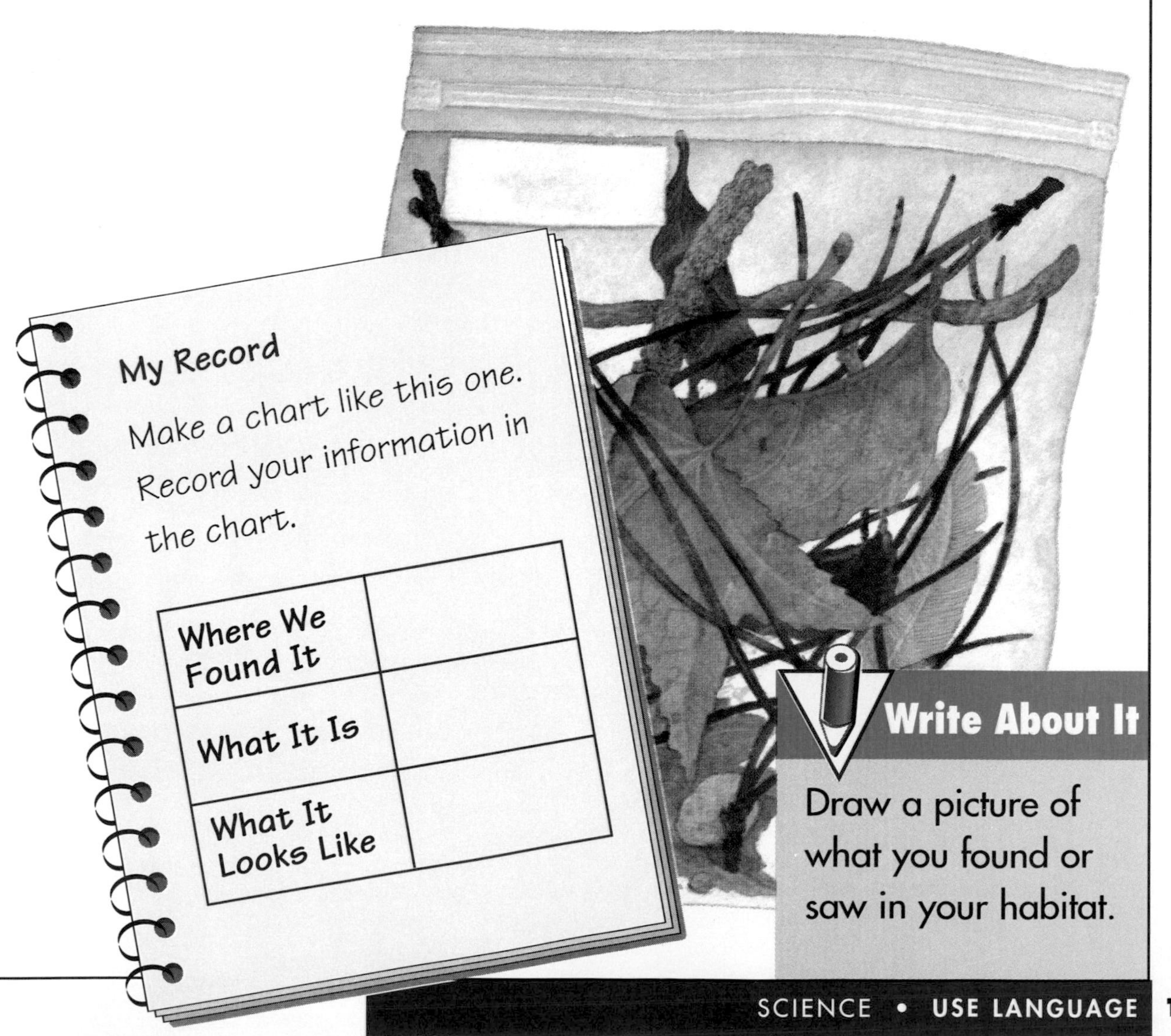

Write About It

Draw a picture of what you found or saw in your habitat.

Children save a rain forest.

Half of the earth's plants and animals live in rain forests like the one in the picture. For many plants and animals, the rain forest is the only habitat in which they can live. The rain forest also makes oxygen for all of us to breathe.

People are cutting down and burning many rain forests. Scientists think that the rain forests will be gone in 100 years. Once a rain forest is gone, it is gone forever.

Thousands of children from all over the world want to save the rain forests. They are collecting pennies and earning money to buy pieces of a rain forest in Costa Rica. This is the Children's Rainforest. No one can cut it down or burn it.

Word Bank

flowers
frogs
insects
monkeys
parrots

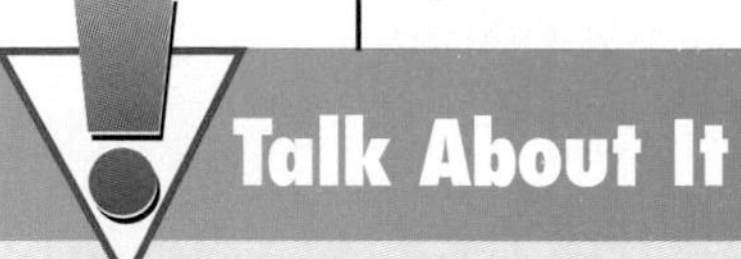

Talk About It

What lives in a rain forest?

Why are rain forests important?

Endangered and Extinct Animals

Some animals die when their environment changes. They become **endangered.** Only a few are left. When all of the animals die, they become **extinct.** Then none are left.

When cities grew larger, ▶ the habitat of the **California condor** was destroyed. Now only a few California condors live in North America.

When people built new houses and buildings in Florida, **crocodiles** lost much of their habitat. People also killed many crocodiles to make clothes from their skins. Today, laws protect crocodiles. ▼

When people cut down the forests ▶ in China to make farmland, the **giant pandas** could not find enough bamboo to eat. Now only a few giant pandas live in China.

When people cut down forests in Asia and Africa to sell the wood, **leopards** could not find enough to eat. Now only a few leopards live in Asia and Africa. ▼

Think About It

What kinds of changes can harm animals?

What do you think people can do to help save endangered animals?

How can you help?

Many groups work to help the environment. You can find out about them at the library. Ask the librarian for the *Encyclopedia of Associations.*

You can write to some groups to learn about what they do. Here are the names of some groups.

The Children's Rainforest
P. O. Box 936
Lewiston, Maine 04240

Kids Against Pollution (KAP)
Tenakill School
275 High Street
Closter, New Jersey 07624

The Nature Conservancy
1815 North Lynn Street
Arlington, Virginia 22209

World Wildlife Fund
1250 24th Street NW
Washington, DC 20037

Here is a letter one student wrote.

1524 Green Street
Evanston, IL 60201
June 10, 1996

The Children's Rainforest
P.O. Box 936
Lewiston, Maine 04240

Dear Sir or Madam:

Today I read an article about the Children's Rainforest. I would like to know more about your group. Please send me information on how you help save the rain forest. Please tell me how I can help.

Sincerely,
Alex Tenorio

Write About It

Choose an environmental group that interests you. Write a letter to the group. Ask how the group helps the environment. Ask what you can do to help.

This Land Is Your Land

by Woody Guthrie

This land is your land;
This land is my land.
From California
to the New York Island,
From the redwood forest
to the Gulf Stream waters,
This land was made for you and me.

Try It Out

Pretend you are a songwriter. Add a verse to Woody Guthrie's song. What parts of this land would you name in it?

Tell what you learned.

CHAPTER 11

1. How does building a city change the environment?
2. Draw a picture of an animal in its habitat. Write about the animal's habitat.
3. Share the information you receive from the environmental group with the class. Plan what your next step will be in helping to protect the environment.
4. What is the most interesting thing you learned in this chapter? Why?

CHAPTER 12

Pollution

Tell what you know.

What is pollution?

How do people cause pollution?

Word Bank

garbage
litter
smoke
trash

Talk About It

What kinds of pollution do you see in your community?

How do people help stop it?

Water Pollution

Some pollution affects water. **Water pollution** happens when anything harmful is added to our lakes, rivers, and oceans. What can be done to prevent water pollution?

▲
People can stop throwing cans, bottles, and garbage into lakes, rivers, and oceans.

▲
Factories can stop dumping their dirty water into rivers and lakes. Factories can also make sure the water they dump is cool. Often it is very hot. Plants and animals cannot live in very hot water.

Farmers can use less harmful materials to grow their crops. Rivers and lakes can become polluted when it rains and these harmful materials are washed into them.

Cities can build sewage treatment plants. These plants clean water before it goes into rivers and lakes.

Think About It

What can you do to prevent water pollution?

How clean is the air?

Some pollution affects air. **Air pollution** happens when anything harmful is added to the air we breathe. Do this experiment with a partner to see how clean our air is.

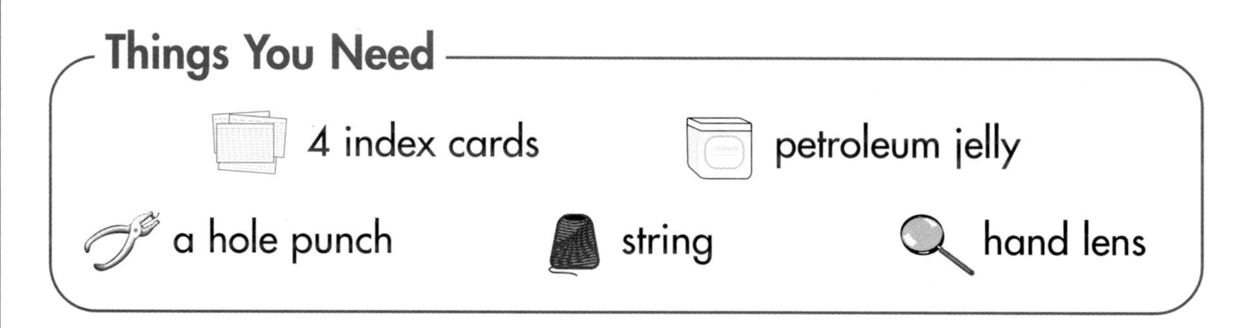

Follow these steps.

1. Write a number on each card.

2. Punch a hole at one end of each card. Tie a long piece of string through the hole to use as a hanger.

3. Spread a thin layer of petroleum jelly on one side of each card.

4. Hang each card in a different place: at school, at home, or outdoors in a place protected from rain.

5. Collect the cards at the end of one week. Use a hand lens to look closely at each card. Tell what you see.

Talk About It

What places seem to have the most air pollution?

What places seem to have the cleanest air?

What can you recycle?

When you **recycle** something, you use it again. Did you know you can recycle garbage? You can use a paper bag again instead of throwing it out. Or you can put some garbage in a recycling bin.

Garbage keeps piling up, and there are fewer places to put it. Recycling garbage helps prevent pollution.

You can recycle paper. Used paper becomes cardboard and paper bags.

You can recycle metal cans. Used metal cans become new cans.

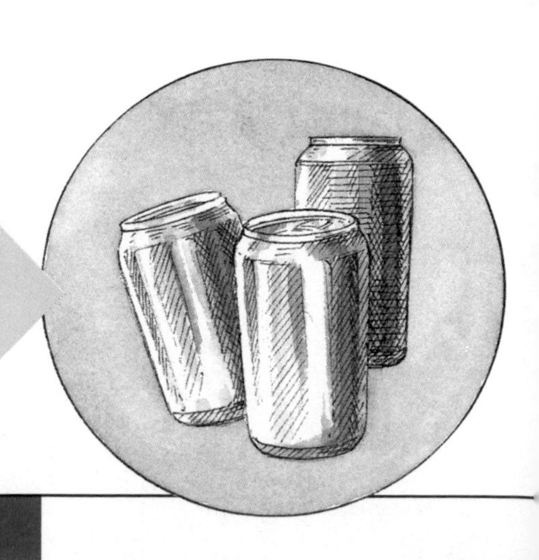

You can recycle plastic bottles. Used plastic bottles become park benches.

You can recycle glass bottles. Used glass becomes new glass.

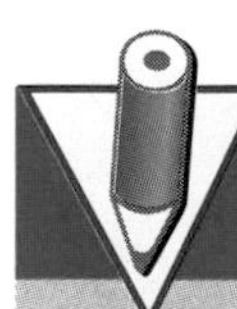

Write About It

List everything you throw away for one day. Circle things that you could recycle.

What can you do about pollution?

You can throw away less trash. You can use less paper. You can reuse things you might have thrown away. You can recycle metal, glass, paper, and plastic.

You can clean up your environment. You can pick up litter and throw it into garbage cans. You can plant trees and plants.

You can plan a clean-up project for your school. You can work together with your classmates to decide what needs to be cleaned up. You can ask other students in the school to help.

You can tell people how you feel about pollution. You can write letters to government officials. You can write to groups that care about the environment. You can ask them how you can help.

Write About It

Work with a group. What will you do about pollution? Write a plan. What will you do first? What will you do next?

Linda's Invention

by Dina Anastasio

Reader's Tip
Here's a story about what one girl does about pollution. Read to find out what Linda does for her neighborhood.

Strategy Tip:
Use Clues from the Sentence and Art
Use the picture and the words around the word *stoop* to figure out what it means.

It was a hot day in the city. Linda and her friends were sitting on the stoop in front of an apartment building.

After a while Linda got up, walked to the curb, and looked down.

"This city is a mess," she said. "You can hardly see the street anymore. Before long we won't be able to find the cars, or the people, or even the buildings. This city is really a mess!"

Linda's friends nodded, but said nothing.

"Don't you *care?*" Linda asked.

Again, Linda's friends said nothing.

Strategy Tip: Identify Story Problem

Most stories have a problem that needs to be solved. What problem does Linda see? Think about how the problem might be solved.

Strategy Tip: Stop and Think
Are Linda's friends interested in her idea to invent something? How do you know?

"Well, I care," Linda said. "And I'm going to do something about it. I'm going to invent something that will clean up every piece of garbage on this street."

"Sure," said Luis, yawning.

"It's impossible," said Ann without looking up.

"Great idea," said Diane, trying hard not to laugh.

Linda's friends had heard it all before. Linda was *always* going to invent something.

When it was hot, Linda was going to invent a machine that would keep her cool.

When she was sad, Linda was going to invent a machine that would hug her and make her laugh.

When she had nothing to do, Linda was going to invent her very own roller coaster.

Language Tip: Vocabulary
A *roller coaster* is a ride people go on for fun.

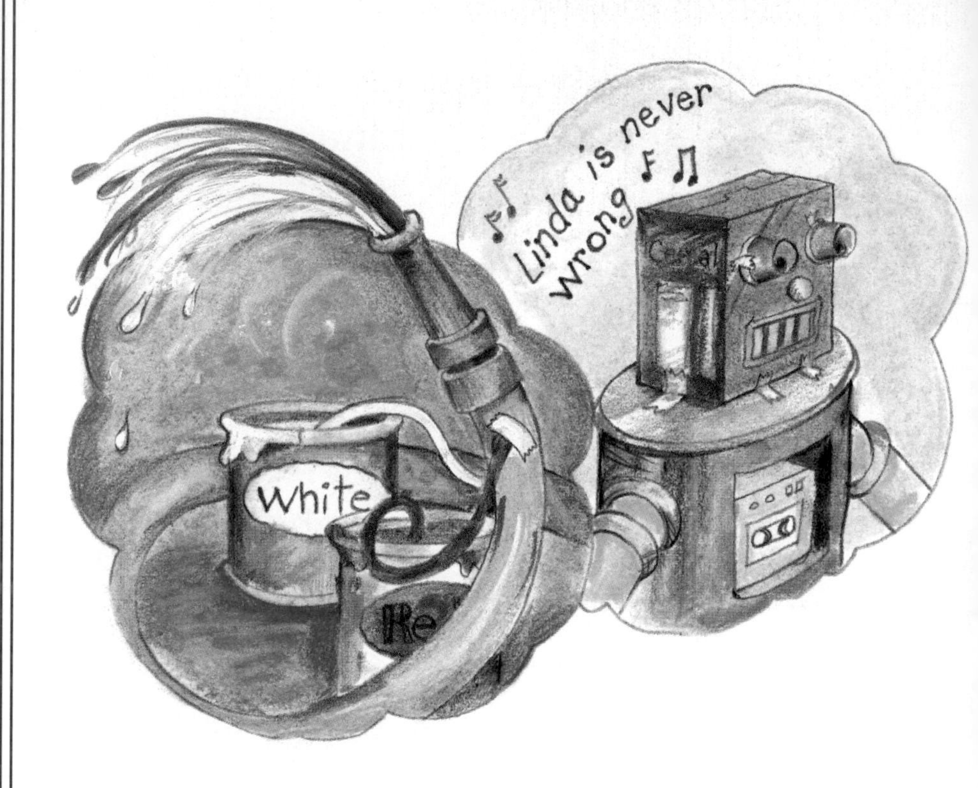

One day Linda was going to invent a fire hose that sprayed red-and-white water.

And the next day she was going to invent a robot that sang "Linda is never wrong, Linda is never wrong."

But Linda never invented anything.

Strategy Tip: Stop and Think
Why do Linda's friends think she will not invent anything?

"All right," said Linda. "You just wait!" And she ran into the apartment building.

Linda did not come out to play the next day, or the day after that.

"Maybe she's sick," said Luis.

"Maybe she went to her uncle's," said Ann.

"Maybe she's inventing a machine to clean up the streets," said Diane. Then everyone laughed. They all knew that Linda would never invent anything.

Language Tip: Possessives
Uncle's is a way of saying "uncle's home" or "uncle's place."

Early the next morning Linda came out of the building. She was carrying a big box. The top of the box had a large hole cut out of it. Above the hole were written the words "THE GARBAGE GAME." Under the hole were the words "TOSS IT IN AND WIN!"

Linda put the box on the sidewalk next to the street. Then she walked back to the stoop and sat down next to her friends.

"What's that?" asked Luis.

"It's my invention," Linda said.

Linda's friends looked at the box and laughed.

"That's silly," said Ann. "How's that going to clean up our street?"

"Just wait," said Linda.

"We'll have to wait for months," laughed Diane.

Linda and her friends sat on the stoop and waited.

Language Tip: Contractions
Hole's stands for two words, *hole* and *is*. *It's* stands for two words, *it* and *is*.

At 10 o'clock Luis went upstairs to get an apple. After he had finished eating it, he tossed it into the box.

"That's really a silly game," he said. "It's much too easy. Anybody can hit that hole."

Linda didn't say anything.

At 11 a piece of paper floated by. Diane picked it up and tossed it into the box.

"The hole's too big," she said. "It's impossible to miss."

Linda didn't say anything.

At 12 a young boy rode by on his bike. He was peeling a banana. When he saw the box, he stopped and threw the peel into it. Then he said, "What do I win?"

"Look at the clean sidewalk," said Linda.

The boy looked. Then he shrugged and got back on his bike. As he turned the corner, he said, "That's a very silly game."

The next four people who came by tossed their garbage into the box. Linda didn't say anything.

But Luis did. "I see," he said. "The hole is supposed to be big. That way no one can miss."

Linda smiled.

"The sidewalk *is* pretty clean," said Ann.

Linda smiled again.

Strategy Tip: Stop and Think
Do you think Linda's invention is working? Why?

"Not a bad invention," said Diane.

Linda kept right on smiling.

No one said anything for a long time. They were looking at the sidewalk. Then Luis leaned back and said, "You know, it's nice."

"Yes," Linda said. "It's very nice."

Reader's Tip
What can we learn from Linda and her friends?

Danger Sign

By Pat Moon

The notice said

WARNING!
THIS WATER IS POLLUTED
DO NOT FISH OR SWIM
THE OWNERS ARE NOT RESPONSIBLE
FOR LOSS OF LIFE OR LIMB

So we gathered up our swimming gear
That we'd no longer need
And wondered should we tell them
That otters cannot read.

Try It Out

Think of ways to tell people how they can "Save the Water." Work with a few friends. Make posters. Hang them at school. Make buttons. Give them to friends. Put on a play.

Tell what you learned.

1. Draw a picture of Linda's street before her invention. Draw a picture of Linda's street after her invention. Tell how the street changed.

2. List three things people do to prevent pollution.

3. Make a chart like this one. Write items you can recycle under each head.

metal	glass	plastic	paper

4. What have you learned about pollution that you want to teach someone younger than you?

Writer's Workshop

Follow these steps to be a good writer.

1 Prewriting

Choose a topic.

List your ideas.

Ask friends for ideas.

Look in books for ideas.

Writing Ideas	
my community	movies
my best friend	my favorite foods
my family	places to live
zoo animals	pets
soccer	computer games

Decide what you want to write.

Do you want to write a story?

Do you want to explain something?

Do you want to describe something?

Do you want to tell how you feel?

Focus on your topic.

Use a graphic organizer.

Focus on one idea.

Find details about your topic.

Look for information in books and magazines.

Ask people for information.

Think about how things look, smell, feel, sound, and taste.

2 Drafting

Get what you need.
Get paper and pencils.
Get your graphic organizer.
Sit in a comfortable place.

Set a goal.
How much will you write now?

Read your notes.
What do you want to say first?

Keep writing.
Write down all your ideas. Don't worry about spelling and punctuation now.

3 Revising

I think I need a better beginning.

Read what you wrote.
Ask yourself:

Does my story have a beginning,
a middle, and an end?
Is my information correct?
What parts should I keep?
What parts should I leave out?

Talk with someone.
Show your writing to a friend
or your teacher.
Do your readers understand
your writing?

 Proofreading

Check your spelling.
Look in a dictionary or ask for help.

Look for capital letters.

Look for correct punctuation.

Make a new copy.

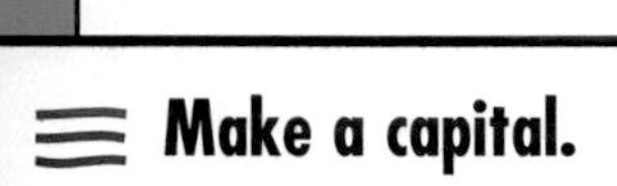

- ≡ **Make a capital.**
- / **Make a small letter.**
- ∧ **Add something.**
- **Take out something.**
- ⊙ **Add a period.**
- ¶ **Make a new paragraph.**

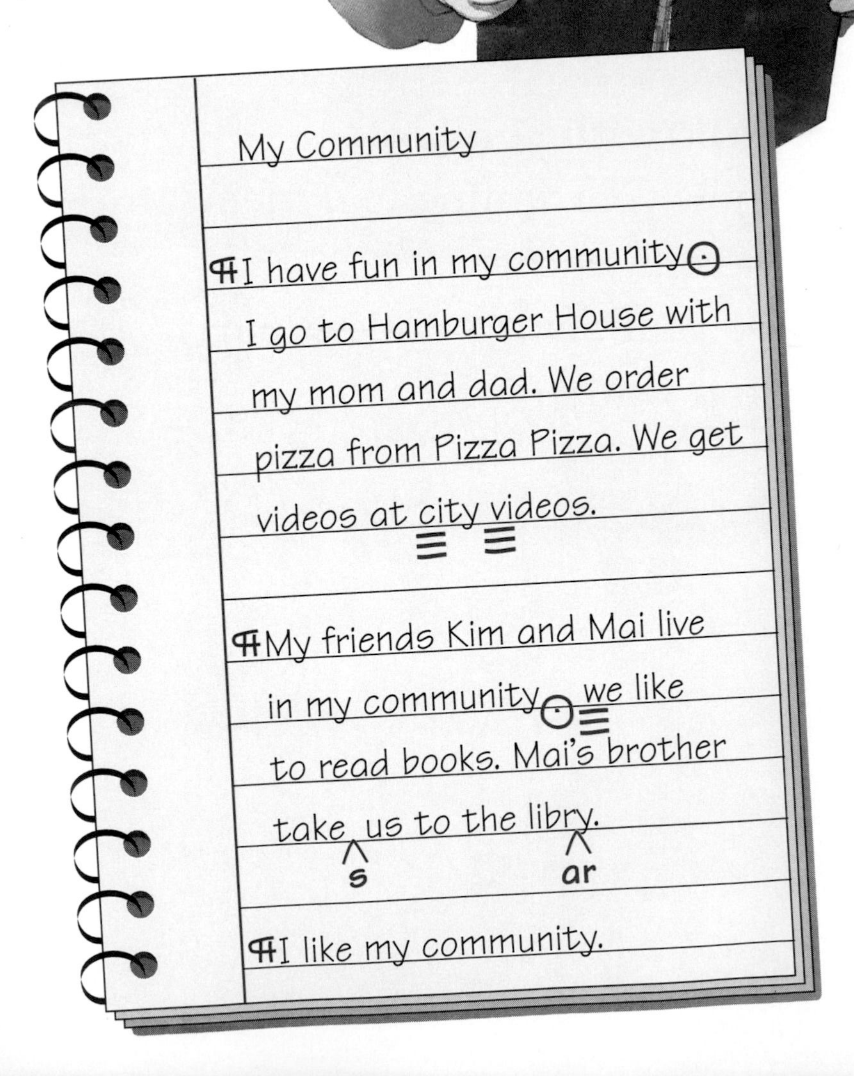

5 Presenting

Share your writing.

Read it aloud to your family or classmates.

Make a book. Lend the book to your family or classmates.

My Community

I have fun in my community. I go to Hamburger House with my mom and dad. We order pizza from Pizza Pizza. We get videos at City Videos.

My friends Kim and Mai live in my community. We like to read books. Mai's brother takes us to the library.

I like my community.

What a Good Writer Can Do

- I can plan before I write.
- I can write about real things.
- I can write stories with a beginning, a middle, and an end.
- I can ask others to read my work.
- I can write in complete sentences.
- I can put periods at the ends of sentences.
- I can make my handwriting easy to read.